Praise for other books by Michael W Lucas

FreeBSD Mastery: Storage Essentials

"If you're a FreeBSD (or Linux, or Unix) sysadmin, then you need this book; it has a *lot* of hard-won knowledge, and will save your butt more than you'll be comfortable admitting. If you've read anything else by Lucas, you also know we need him writing more books. Do the right thing and buy this now." – *Slashdot*

"There's plenty of coverage of GEOM, GELI, GDBE, and the other technologies specific to FreeBSD. I for one did not know how GEOM worked, with its consumer/producer model – and I imagine it's complex to dive into when you've got a broken machine next to you. If you are administering FreeBSD systems, especially ones that deal with dedicated storage, you will find this useful." — *DragonFlyBSD Digest*

Networking for Systems Administrators

"There is a lot of useful information packed into this book. I recommend it!"—*Sunday Morning Linux Review, episode 145*

After reading this book, you'll have a strong footing in networking. Lucas explains concepts in practical ways; he makes sure to teach tools in both Unix/Linux and Windows; and he gives you the terms you'll use to explain what you're seeing to the network folks. Along the way there's a lot of hard-won knowledge sprinkled throughout…" – *Slashdot*

Sudo Mastery

"It's awesome, it's Lucas, it's sudo. Buy it now." – *Slashdot*

"Michael W Lucas has always been one of my favorite authors because he brings exceptional narrative to information that has the potential to be rather boring. *Sudo Mastery* is no exception." – *Chris Sanders, author of Practical Packet Analysis*

Absolute OpenBSD, 2nd Edition

"Michael Lucas has done it again." – *cryptednets.org*

"After 13 years of using OpenBSD, I learned something new and useful!" – *Peter Hessler, OpenBSD Journal*

"This is truly an excellent book. It's full of essential material on OpenBSD presented with a sense of humor and an obvious deep knowledge of how this OS works. If you're coming to this book from a Unix background of any kind, you're going to find what you need to quickly become fluent in OpenBSD – both how it works and how to manage it with expertise. I doubt that a better book on OpenBSD could be written." — *Sandra Henry-Stocker, ITWorld.com*

"It quickly becomes clear that Michael actually uses OpenBSD and is not a hired gun with a set word count to satisfy... In short, this is not a drive-by book and you will not find any hand waving." – *Michael Dexter, callfortesting.org*

DNSSEC Mastery

"When Michael descends on a topic and produces a book, you can expect the result to contain loads of useful information, presented along with humor and real-life anecdotes so you will want to explore the topic in depth on your own systems." — *Peter Hansteen, author of The Book of PF*

"Pick up this book if you want an easy way to dive into DNSSEC." — *psybermonkey.net*

SSH Mastery

"…one of those technical books that you wouldn't keep on your bookshelf. It's one of the books that will have its bindings bent, and many pages bookmarked sitting near the keyboard." — *Steven K Hicks, SKH:TEC*

"…SSH Mastery is a title that Unix users and system administrators like myself will want to keep within reach…" — *Peter Hansteen, author of The Book of PF*

"This stripping-down of the usual tech-book explanations gives it the immediacy of extended documentation on the Internet. Not the multipage how-to articles used as vehicles for advertising, but an in-depth presentation from someone who used OpenSSH to do a number of things, and paid attention while doing it." — *DragonFlyBSD Digest*

Network Flow Analysis

"Combining a great writing style with lots of technical info, this book provides a learning experience that's both fun and interesting. Not too many technical books can claim that." — *;login: Magazine, October 2010*

"This book is worth its weight in gold, especially if you have to deal with a shoddy ISP who always blames things on your network." — *Utahcon.com*

"The book is a comparatively quick read and will come in handy when troubleshooting and analyzing network problems." — *Dr. Dobbs*

"Network Flow Analysis is a pick for any library strong in network administration and data management. It's the first to show system administrators how to assess, analyze and debut a network using flow analysis, and comes from one of the best technical writers in the networking and security environments." — *Midwest Book Review*

Absolute FreeBSD, 2nd Edition

"I am happy to say that Michael Lucas is probably the best system administration author I've read. I am amazed that he can communicate top-notch content with a sense of humor, while not offending the reader or sounding stupid. When was the last time you could physically feel yourself getting smarter while reading a book? If you are a beginning to average FreeBSD user, Absolute FreeBSD 2nd Ed (AF2E) will deliver that sensation in spades. Even more advanced users will find plenty to enjoy." — *Richard Bejtlich, CSO, MANDIANT, and TaoSecurity blogger*

"Master practitioner Lucas organizes features and functions to make sense in the development environment, and so provides aid and comfort to new users, novices, and those with significant experience alike." — *SciTech Book News*

"…reads well as the author has a very conversational tone, while giving you more than enough information on the topic at hand. He drops in jokes and honest truths, as if you were talking to him in a bar." — *Technology and Me Blog*

Cisco Routers for the Desperate, 2nd Edition

"If only Cisco Routers for the Desperate had been on my bookshelf a few years ago! It would have definitely saved me many hours of searching for configuration help on my Cisco routers." — *Blogcritics Magazine*

"For me, reading this book was like having one of the guys in my company who lives and breathes Cisco sitting down with me for a day and explaining everything I need to know to handle problems or issues likely to come my way. There may be many additional things I could potentially learn about my Cisco switches, but likely few I'm likely to encounter in my environment." — *IT World*

"This really ought to be the book inside every Cisco Router box for the very slim chance things go goofy and help is needed 'right now.'" — *MacCompanion*

Absolute OpenBSD

"My current favorite is Absolute OpenBSD: Unix for the Practical Paranoid by Michael W. Lucas from No Starch Press. Anyone should be able to read this book, download OpenBSD, and get it running as quickly as possible." — *Infoworld*

"I recommend Absolute OpenBSD to all programmers and administrators working with the OpenBSD operating system (OS), or considering it." — *UnixReview*

"Absolute OpenBSD by Michael Lucas is a broad and mostly gentle introduction into the world of the OpenBSD operating system. It is sufficiently complete and deep to give someone new to OpenBSD a solid footing for doing real work and the mental tools for further exploration… The potentially boring topic of systems administration is made very readable and even fun by the light tone that Lucas uses." — *Chris Palmer, President, San Francisco OpenBSD Users Group*

PGP & GPG

"...The World's first user-friendly book on email privacy...unless you're a cryptographer, or never use email, you should read this book." — *Len Sassaman, CodeCon Founder*

"An excellent book that shows the end-user in an easy to read and often entertaining style just about everything they need to know to effectively and properly use PGP and OpenPGP." — *Slashdot*

"PGP & GPG is another excellent book by Michael Lucas. I thoroughly enjoyed his other books due to their content and style. PGP & GPG continues in this fine tradition. If you are trying to learn how to use PGP or GPG, or at least want to ensure you are using them properly, read PGP & GPG." — *TaoSecurity*

Tarsnap Mastery

"If you use any nix-type system, and need offsite backups, then you need Tarsnap. If you want to use Tarsnap efficiently, you need Tarsnap Mastery." *–Sunday Morning Linux Review episode 148*

Praise for Allan Jude

"[Cloud vs bare metal] is all about tradeoffs and understanding your requirements. Allan's BSDCan talk from a few years ago was great." — *Simon L. B. Nielsen, Google SRE*

"Allan's work on the ZFS section of the handbook was really helpful and severely reduced the need for Googling things." — *Marie Helene Kvello-Aune, FreeBSD/ZFS User*

FreeBSD Mastery:

ZFS

Michael W Lucas
Allan Jude

We dedicate *FreeBSD Mastery: ZFS* to our good friend
Paul Schenkeveld
who sadly passed away as we wrote this book.

Brief Contents

Complete Contents

Acknowledgements

The authors would like to thank all the people who have helped us with this book in one way or another. That includes a whole bunch of people on the FreeBSD mailing lists, lots of folks on social media, and every customer who's ever damaged their filesystem.

We'd also like to thank the technical reviewers who took time from their lives to give us feedback: Brooks Davis, John W. De Boskey, Alexey Dokuchaev, Julien Elischer, Pedro Giffuni, Marie Helene Kvello-Aune, Kurt Jaeger, Alexander Leidinger, Johannes Meixner, and Alexander Motin. We might not *enjoy* being told exactly how we're wrong, but we do *appreciate* it.

Lucas would like to specifically thank iXsystems for their excellent test hardware, his wife Liz for everything, and Costco for their ultra-economy-size ibuprofen.

Jude would like to thank the *BSD community for welcoming him so warmly, with special thanks to his mentors Benedict Reuschling, Warren Block, and Eitan Adler, as well as Dru Lavigne, Devin Teske, George Neville-Neil, and Matt Ahrens.

Lucas would also like to thank Jude for that effusive acknowledgement of specific cool people in the FreeBSD community, thus making him look comparatively churlish. But he's thanked specific FreeBSDers before, so it could be worse.

Chapter 0: Introduction

Much of our systems administration training focuses on filesystems. A computer's filesystem dictates so much of its performance and behavior. Over the last decades we've rebuilt entire systems because a major filesystem was configured incorrectly, or the filesystem chosen wasn't suitable for the task, or because subtle filesystem corruption spread throughout our files and now we couldn't trust even the basic programs the operating system had shipped with. Anyone who's been a sysadmin more than a few years has learned how to repair filesystems, rebuild filesystems, work around bugs from vexing to nearly lethal, rearrange disks to support filesystem limitations, and swear extensively at filesystems in no fewer than nine languages.

Some of today's most popular filesystems are, in computing scale, ancient. We discard hardware because it's five years old and too slow to be borne—then put a 30-year-old filesystem on its replacement. Even more modern filesystems like extfs, UFS2, and NTFS use older ideas at their core.

The Z File System, or ZFS, is here to change all that.

What is ZFS?

ZFS is a modern filesystem built with the core idea that the filesystem should be able to guarantee data integrity. ZFS computes a checksum for every piece of data on disk, so it can identify when the storage

1

media has experienced an error and damaged the data. It performs the same cryptographic signatures on all of the metadata. When—not if—the underlying hardware has a problem or just misfires, ZFS realizes that the data it has retrieved doesn't match its records and can take action. ZFS even automatically corrects discovered errors! ZFS refuses to serve data it knows to be corrupt.

Filesystem designers had these ideas 30 years ago, but the hardware of the time couldn't perform this amount of error checking with reasonable performance. The creators of ZFS looked at current hardware as well as where hardware was going, and decided that ZFS would take full advantage of emerging hardware. The result is a filesystem that's not only more reliable than traditional filesystems, but often faster.

Today, it seems that traditional filesystems were written with a "good enough for now" philosophy. Many filesystems suffered from arbitrary size limits, which sufficed for five years, or ten, or even 20 but eventually required rewriting and reworking. Many older filesystems couldn't handle partitions larger than two gigabytes, which these days is smaller than a flash drive you'll get for free attached to a bottle opener. (And really, you picked that up because you wanted the bottle opener.) But in the early 1980s, when UFS was first released, two gigabytes was a ridiculously large amount of storage that would cost many millions of dollars. Filesystems like FAT needed to efficiently use the space on 360 KB floppy disks. UFS was "good enough for now," and for some time to come.

ZFS is deliberately designed to survive the foreseeable future and more. Many new filesystems use 64-bit identifiers and indexes internally, so they'll be usable without change for the next ten or 20 years. ZFS use 128-bit identifiers internally, giving it enough capacity to work on storage systems for the next several millennia. The Enterprise's computer on *Star Trek* probably runs ZFS. Future sysadmins who must deal with disks, partitions, and files that exceed ZFS' built-in constraints will lump us together in history with the cavemen and the first interstellar travelers.

Strictly speaking, ZFS is not just a filesystem. It's a combination filesystem and volume manager. Combining these two functions in one set of software does impose certain limitations, which we'll talk about later—but it also makes some very interesting things possible. ZFS, being aware of exactly where data is going on the disk, can arrange files and stripes optimally, from top to bottom. ZFS can use secondary fast storage as special-purpose caches, further enhancing performance.

FreeBSD Mastery: ZFS Essentials takes you through what you must know to run this modern, high-performance, future-proof filesystem.

ZFS History

Matt Ahrens and Jeff Bonwick created ZFS for Sun Microsystems' Solaris® operating system. While Sun sold systems of all sizes, its main focus was high-end server hardware. Sun hardware drove most of the world's large databases. Sun offered the ZFS source code to the world under its Common Development and Distribution License (CDDL). People began porting ZFS to other operating systems, including FreeBSD, and contributing changes back to Sun.

Then Oracle bought Sun Microsystems. While Oracle has some open source software, such as MySQL, most of its software is proprietary. Oracle brought ZFS development fully in-house and ceased providing source code under any open source license.

But the ZFS code was already out in public, and under the CDDL license terms, Oracle couldn't stop people from using it. Various open source projects spun up their own ZFS development efforts.

Today, the OpenZFS Project (http://open-zfs.org) is the main coordinator of the open source version of ZFS. OpenZFS brings together ZFS developers from many companies and operating systems, including Linux, OS X, Illumos, and FreeBSD. Matt Ahrens leads the project.

Unlike the rest of FreeBSD, ZFS has a restrictive license. The CDDL limits one's ability to file patent lawsuits, and contributions back to ZFS are automatically put under the CDDL. FreeBSD's 2-clause BSD license permits anyone to use the code for anything, including patent lawsuits. But the CDDL permits reuse, redistribution, and changing of the code, so the code is usable by anyone in any common enterprise environment. If you want to base a product on ZFS or include ZFS in another product, however, consult a lawyer.

Prerequisites

This book is written for FreeBSD systems administrators interested in ZFS. We assume that you are familiar with the basics of FreeBSD, including installing, configuring users, and managing GEOM-based storage. You should know what a "storage provider" is and why we use that term. If you're uncertain of your skills, you might pick up a book like *Absolute FreeBSD* (No Starch Press, 2007) or other *FreeBSD Mastery* titles to augment your knowledge, or consult the online documentation and man pages.

If you're using OpenZFS on an operating system other than FreeBSD, this book offers a bunch of practical ZFS knowledge and experience you can take advantage of. You'll need to ignore the FreeBSD-specific stuff, but you'll learn how to optimize and manage ZFS.

We have not tested this book against Oracle ZFS. Oracle has taken its closed-source ZFS in its own direction, and you're really better off reading Oracle's official documentation if you must run Oracle Solaris.

You really should know something about disk technologies. FreeBSD's ZFS can run atop any GEOM provider, but running on raw disk offers certain benefits. Running ZFS on a RAID container eliminates those benefits. You should be able to slap a RAID controller into acting as a bunch of disks.

You should also have a test machine for playing with ZFS. Don't buy this book and immediately migrate your main database server to ZFS! Install ZFS on a test machine, then a less critical machine. Experiment with ZFS features until you're confident you can best configure ZFS to support your systems' purposes. While ZFS is fast, no filesystem is so tolerant that a sysadmin cannot configure it to perform poorly.

Where to Use ZFS?

You can use ZFS anywhere, but in some places it won't work well.

ZFS might not be the best choice for certain virtualization systems. We've used more than one Linux KVM-based virtualization system that chokes on ZFS filesystems, and would not be shocked to see other systems have similar issues. Features such as migration between hosts and restoring from an image-based backup can be problematic. You'll want to fully test ZFS on your virtualization system before using it there. Lucas has deployed ZFS on these systems, mind you, but he uses alternative backup and migration strategies.

ZFS is written for modern hardware. It expects that you have at least a few gigabytes of RAM. Embedded systems such as the Raspberry Pi are better suited for traditional filesystems like UFS2.

Certain high-intensity workloads on certain hardware perform better on UFS2 than on ZFS, especially if you have hard drives with actual 512-byte blocks. If you expect to beat the living snot out of your database, test its performance with both UFS2 and ZFS.

ZFS Hardware

Many people recommend high-end hardware for ZFS. We like high-end hardware too. It's nifty. But ZFS works just fine on commodity hardware, so long as you understand the limitations of the hardware. Much of the ZFS documentation you'll find on the Internet includes recommendations that are not applicable to modern ZFS, or not applicable to FreeBSD.

RAM

It's not surprising that Sun's documentation said you needed ECC RAM to use ZFS well. Sun sold high-end servers. But according to Matt Ahrens, "ZFS on a system without ECC is no more dangerous than any other filesystem on a system with ECC." ZFS' built-in error correction compensates for most but not all memory-induced errors.

The generic arguments in favor of ECC RAM are still valid, of course. A machine with non-ECC memory can suffer memory corruption, and it's possible for some of those errors to get to disk. That would happen regardless of the filesystem you're using, however, and ZFS checksums offer a hope of identifying the problem. If you're running a high-availability service, you want ECC for all of the usual reasons. But your ZFS laptop or home movie server will function just fine with normal RAM.

RAID Controllers

Do not use a hardware RAID controller. Ever. Running ZFS on top of a hardware RAID device creates a configuration with all the disadvantages of RAID and all the disadvantages of ZFS. Use a non-RAID host bus adapter (HBA) for your disk controller.

All RAID is software RAID. Your hardware RAID controller runs a custom operating system to perform RAID tasks, and in the process obscures the hardware from the operating system. This made sense back in the early days of widespread commercial computing, when consumer operating systems could not be trusted to manage storage. Spend three seconds contemplating running OS-level software RAID on Windows 3.1, and you'll understand why hardware RAID became so ubiquitous.

Our operating systems have gotten better. Our hardware is billions of times more powerful. The environment has changed.

ZFS is designed for direct access to the hardware. It deliberately stores critical metadata on multiple disks. It watches those disks for errors, and makes decisions based on those errors. A hardware RAID device hides all of this worrisome detail from the operating system, eliminating ZFS' ability to heal itself. Hardware RAID presents no competing abilities.

Rebuilding a ZFS array is much faster than rebuilding a RAID array, thanks to ZFS' integration of redundancy with the filesystem. If you manage redundancy with hardware RAID, you lose that speed.

Many RAID controllers will not let you use disks without some sort of RAID, however. Even if you configure the controller to have "just a bunch of disks," or JBOD, these controllers actually format each drive as a single disk RAID-0. This masks certain information, such as block size and many disk errors, from the operating system. Worse, disks used on such a controller are readable only by this brand of controller—and sometimes, only by this model of RAID controller! Using such a RAID controller for ZFS means you won't be able to move these hard drives to another machine without reformatting them, unless the new box happens to have the exact same RAID card. This eliminates all of ZFS' pool portability.

Some hardware RAID cards can be reflashed to be JBOD controllers. A bad flash might brick your RAID card. As neither of the authors will use hardware RAID again, we take that risk.

If you're condemned to use hardware RAID, probably because you were a very bad person in a previous life, present the operating system with single disks. If the RAID controller insists on formatting each disk as a RAID-0, you're stuck. Disable "write back" mode on the controller; otherwise, the controller's write cache can corrupt your filesystem. Resign yourself to increased complexity, reduced performance, and added risk. Be sure to document all this in an email to management, so when the inevitable failure happens, you get the tiny pleasure of saying "I told you so" to compensate for the pain of restoring from backup.

Host bus adapters are much less expensive than RAID cards—not only in money, but in time. Use them.

SATA vs. SAS vs. SSD

Data storage devices come in a variety of types. ZFS can use SAS drives, SATA drives, spinning platters, SSD devices, or any other storage media supported by the operating system.

That's not to say that the drives are equivalent. SAS drives can usually last much longer than SATA drives under the same load. Flash drives are much faster than any kind of spinning disk. ZFS can store data on any of these. Base your choice of drive hardware on your organization's needs, not on ZFS.

ZFS can make special use of extra-fast storage as read and write caches. If you can add a couple of solid state disks to your SAS or SATA-based storage array, you can vastly accelerate ZFS' performance.

Disk Redundancy

It's not uncommon for a storage array to lose several disks simultaneously. A power surge can damage multiple disks. An intensive array rebuild stresses the remaining disks. Heat can build up on one side of the shelf. ZFS supports multiple redundancy scenarios for exactly these reasons.

If you buy a whole bunch of identical disks, they might all be made on the same day or in the same batch. A bad day at the manufacturing plant can bite you hard. Sadly, disk retailers can't ship you drives made on different days or in different batches. The best you can do is to have each array include drives made by multiple manufacturers.

Physical Redundancy

FreeBSD supports multipath storage, allowing you to work around many hardware problems. Rearranging your hardware might increase the system's availability and reliability. If you have two external disk arrays, perhaps use a disk from each array in your mirrored pair. This way, if a disk array's power supply dies, each mirror still has one active disk. When the failed array is restored, the mirrors automatically recover. As this is specialty equipment, we discuss multipath in *FreeBSD Mastery: Advanced ZFS*.

Look at your hardware before installation. Consider how it might fail, and how proper arrangement of your kit might prevent outages.

Disk Installation and Labeling

No, not using a label machine and pasting a little sticker on each hard drive. The glue on those things never sticks (although you should physically label your disks). FreeBSD supports Globally Unique ID (GUID) Partition Tables (GPT) labels, letting you put arbitrary logical markers on a hard drive or a partition. If a storage device has a problem, FreeBSD announces the problem and identifies the troubled unit by device name or device node. While it's nice to know that disk /dev/da239 has a problem, you must track that back to a physical device. Many ZFS users have machines with many hard drives, exacerbating the issue.

FreeBSD tools let you get the serial number of a failed drive. Depending on your hardware, however, you might have to physically examine each drive to identify its serial number. This usually involves either opening a case or pulling individual drives out of a disk array. This is tedious, unpleasant, and most often interrupts service.

If you prepare during installation, you can zero right in on a failed disk—even a disk at a remote facility. Jude runs a lot of very dense storage arrays in locations all over the world, and uses this scheme to keep hard drive maintenance from overwhelming him.

Come up with a naming and numbering scheme for your storage arrays. Many storage arrays have a standard naming scheme, often printed on the equipment. If your equipment already has numbered shelves, use that numbering. Otherwise, make simple rules like "shelf 0 is always at the top and disk 0 is always at the left." You might use the prefix "f" for the front and "b" for the back, or whatever works for you.

Note the serial number of each drive as you install it in the array. Physically label each drive tray as you install it by physical location and serial number. Yes, this is tedious—but you'll eventually need this information. You can do this work in peace and quiet at your own pace, or you can desperately rush through it during an artificially prolonged and unnecessarily stressful outage.

Now either install FreeBSD or boot live media. Use `camcontrol devlist` to get a list of all your storage devices, then run `diskinfo -v` on each storage device node to get its serial number. (You can also extract serial numbers from `camcontrol(8)`.) This will tell you that, say, disk `/dev/da0` is actually disk 3 on shelf 4.

You now have a list of device nodes and their associated serial numbers, as well as a list of physical locations and serial numbers. Match those up with each other, and then use GPT labels to attach the location and serial number to the disk partition you're using. (See the FreeBSD documentation or *FreeBSD Mastery: Storage Essentials* for details on GPT labels.) GPT labels have a maximum length of 15 characters, so you might have to truncate long serial numbers. In most serial numbers the last digits are most unique, so trim off the front.

Combined, disk 9 in shelf 2, with a serial number of WD-WCAW36477223, might get a label like */dev/gpt/s2d9-AW36477223*.

You want your system to use these labels, and *only* these labels. Disable GPTID and disk ident labels on the system. This avoids confusion later.

With this setup, during a hardware failure now FreeBSD can tell you that the third disk on shelf 4, serial number such-and-such, is bad. Given that information, even the most junior tech at your colocation provider should be able to pull the right disk.[1] Have the tech give you the serial number of the replacement drive before installation, so you can create the proper labels.

Advance planning makes outages much less traumatic. We highly recommend it.

About this Book

This book is for anyone who manages ZFS filesystems or who is curious about what a modern, high-performance filesystem looks like. While it focuses on ZFS on FreeBSD, the general ZFS information applies to any platform running OpenZFS. Parts of this book happen to be applicable to other implementations, such as Oracle ZFS, but you can't assume this book applies to these other implementations.

We really wanted to write a single FreeBSD OpenZFS book, but limitations in the chosen publishing platforms made that impractical. *FreeBSD Mastery: ZFS* covers routine use of ZFS. The next book, *FreeBSD Mastery: Advanced ZFS*, covers online replication, performance tuning, and other topics requiring greater understanding of

---

1   He will probably screw it up, because that's what junior techs do. But give the poor guy a shot.

ZFS. The second book assumes you understand everything in this book, however.

OpenZFS advances constantly. This book is a static entity. What's more, a book that covered every OpenZFS feature would be the size of the print version of the Manhattan telephone book.[2] These books try to offer what the vast majority of sysadmins must know to run ZFS well. If you're looking for a feature we don't discuss, or you have a special edge case we don't cover, definitely check the man pages, the online OpenZFS documentation, and the FreeBSD mailing lists archives and forums.

Book Overview

Chapter 0 is this introduction.

Chapter 1, Introducing ZFS, gives you a pterodon's-eye view of the ZFS software suite. You'll learn how to look at ZFS filesystems and data pools, and understand how the large chunks of ZFS fit together.

Chapter 2, Virtual Devices, takes you through the ZFS' physical redundancy schemes. ZFS supports traditional mirrored disks and concatenated devices, but also offers its own advanced parity-based redundancy, RAID-Z.

Chapter 3, Pools, discusses ZFS storage pools. You'll learn how to assemble virtual devices into pools, how to check pools, and how to manage and query your storage pools.

Chapter 4, Datasets, takes you through what traditionalists would call a filesystem. Except in ZFS, it's not really a filesystem. Yes, you put files in a dataset, but a dataset is so much more.

---

2   See, once upon a time the phone company printed huge books that listed everyone with a phone and their phone number. No, phone numbers didn't change so often, because they were all landlines. But then the dinosaurs knocked the phone lines down, so we went cellular.

Chapter 5, Pool Repairs and Renovations, covers making changes to storage pools. You can expand storage pools with additional disks, repair failed disks, and tweak pools to support new features.

Chapter 6, Disk Space Management, covers one of the most misunderstood parts of using ZFS. Why does your 1 TB drive claim to have 87 TB free? How do you reserve space for some users and limit others? What about this deduplication stuff? This chapter covers all that and more.

Chapter 7, Snapshots and Clones, discusses ZFS' snapshot feature. You can create a point-in-time photograph of a dataset, and refer back to it later. You want a copy of a file as it existed yesterday? Snapshots are your friends. Similarly, clones let you duplicate a filesystem. You'll understand both.

Chapter 8, Installing to ZFS, covers installing FreeBSD to a ZFS. The FreeBSD installer can install a ZFS-based system for you. The installer is always improving, but the real world is more complex than any installation program can possibly expect. Knowing how to install the system exactly the way you want is useful.

Fasten your seat belt and get ready to dive into a filesystem for the 21st century.

Chapter 1: Introducing ZFS

Starting to learn ZFS isn't hard. Install a recent FreeBSD release. Tell the installer you want ZFS. You've started. If you've never worked with ZFS, take a moment and install a new FreeBSD with ZFS on a test system or virtual machine. Don't choose encryption or any of the fancy customization options. This trivial install offers an opportunity to look at some ZFS basics before diving into more complicated setups.

ZFS combines the functions of traditional filesystems and volume managers. As such, it expects to handle everything from the permissions on individual files and which files are in which directories down to tracking which storage devices get used for what purposes and how that storage is arranged. The sysadmin instructs ZFS in arranging disks and files, but ZFS manages the whole storage stack beneath them. This chapter separates the ZFS stack into three layers: filesystems, storage pools, and virtual devices, using a FreeBSD 10.1 host installed with the default ZFS settings.

To orient you, we start at the most visible parts of the storage stack and work our way down. Once you understand how the layers fit together, the rest of this book starts at the foundation and works its way up.

ZFS Datasets

ZFS filesystems aren't exactly analogous to traditional filesystems, and so are called *datasets*. The classic Unix File System (UFS) and its

15

derivatives and work-alikes, such as modern BSD's UFS2 and Linux's extfs, manage filesystems with a variety of programs. You're probably well accustomed to using df(1), newfs(8), mount(8), umount(8), dump(8), restore(8), and similar commands. ZFS absorbs all of these functions in the zfs(8) program, which lets you create, destroy, view, and otherwise spindle ZFS datasets.

Start by viewing existing ZFS datasets with zfs list.

```
# zfs list
NAME                   USED   AVAIL  REFER  MOUNTPOINT
zroot                  429M   13.0G    96K  none
zroot/ROOT             428M   13.0G    96K  none
zroot/ROOT/default     428M   13.0G   428M  /
zroot/tmp              104K   13.0G   104K  /tmp
zroot/usr              428K   13.0G    96K  /usr
...
```

This combines the output of mount(8) and df(1), and should look pretty familiar to anyone who's managed UFS or extfs.

Each dataset has a name. A ZFS dataset name starts with the ZFS storage pool, or *zpool*, the dataset is on. Our first entry is called just plain zroot. This entry represents the pool's *root dataset*, which everything else hangs off of.

The next two columns show amount of space used and available. The pool zroot has used 429 MB and 13 GB free.

The REFER column is special to ZFS. This is the amount of accessible data on the dataset, which is not necessarily the same as the amount of space used. Some ZFS features, such as snapshots, share data between themselves. Our zroot entry has "used" 429 MB, but only refers to 96 KB of data. The pool as a whole has 13 GB free, but 96 KB are accessible through this specific dataset. That's not much. The rest of the space is used for children of this dataset. Chapter 6 gives a detailed discussion of ZFS disk usage. A dataset's children include snapshots, volumes, and child datasets, as you'll see throughout this book.

16

Finally we have the filesystem mount point. The *zroot* ZFS is not mounted.

Look at the second entry, named *zroot/ROOT*. This is a ZFS dataset created for the root filesystem. Like the *zroot* pool, it isn't mounted. It refers 96 KB of data. This apparently isn't used, which seems strange for a root filesystem.

The third entry, *zroot/ROOT/default*, is the current root filesystem. It uses 428 MB of data, and is mounted on /, the Unix root. It refers to 428 MB, meaning that there's that amount of data in this dataset.

Why would ZFS split out this from the root filesystem? ZFS makes it easy to choose between multiple root filesystems. This host runs FreeBSD 10.1, but suppose you must apply some security updates and reboot? Applying operating system patches always afflicts systems administrators with a gut-twisting mix of fear and hope. Even a well-tested upgrade can go wrong and ruin everyone's day. But ZFS lets you clone and snapshot datasets. When you upgrade to FreeBSD 10.1-p1, you could create a new dataset such as *zroot/ROOT/10.1-p1* and tell FreeBSD to use that as the root partition. You either wouldn't mount *zroot/ROOT/default*, or I'd mount it at an alternate location like */oldroot*. If the upgrade goes poorly, reversion is trivial.

The next dataset, *zroot/tmp*, is almost empty. It's mounted at */tmp*. This dataset is the traditional temporary directory.

ZFS Partitions and Properties

ZFS lacks traditional partitions. A partition is a logical subdivision of a disk, filling very specific Logical Block Addresses (LBAs) on a storage device. Partitions have no awareness of the data on the partition. Changing a partition means destroying and (presumably) rebuilding the filesystem on top of it.

Lucas' first thought on seeing a partition-less filesystem was to wonder how he would manage his storage, at all. That's roughly equivalent to the confusion he experiences when, after a long cold Michigan winter, he steps outside and feels natural warm air for the first time in months. Confusion is part of liberation. We learned to administer storage via partitions because we had to, not because partitions are pleasant or because they're the best solution. Running a traditional filesystem without partitions is poor practice, but ZFS is not a traditional filesystem.

ZFS tightly integrates the filesystem and the lower storage layers. This means it can dynamically divide storage space between the various filesystems as needed. While you can set specific size limits on a ZFS filesystem, datasets do not have traditional sizes. If the pool has enough space for a file, you can use it. Where you previously allocated a limited amount of disk space to, say, */var/log*, and thus kept berserk logs from filling your disk, you must now set those limits at the ZFS level.

The amount of space a dataset may use is one example of a ZFS *property*. ZFS supports dozens of dataset properties—for example, the `quota` property controls how large a dataset can grow. Use `zfs(8)` to set a ZFS property.

```
# zfs set quota=2G zroot/var/log
```

View a property with the `zfs get` command.

```
# zfs get quota zroot/var/log
NAME             PROPERTY   VALUE   SOURCE
zroot/var/log    quota         2G   local
```

View all of a dataset's properties with `zfs get all` and the ZFS dataset name.

Chapter 4 explores ZFS properties in detail, while Chapter 6 discusses restricting dataset size.

ZFS Limits

Filesystems have always had maximum sizes and limits. The FAT filesystem we all know and cringe over has required multiple revisions, in part to overcome its maximum size of 32 MB, then 2 GB, then 4 GB. FAT32's 2 TB limit is starting to look a little cramped these days. UFS and ext2/3/4fs have had their own, similarly arbitrary, limits. These limits exist because the filesystem authors had to set a limit somewhere, and chose values that they expected to be good for the next several years. A popular filesystem will remain in use until those limits are reached, however, so systems administrators have needed to repeatedly cope with them.

ZFS advocates claim that ZFS is immune to these arbitrary limits, but that's not *quite* true. ZFS uses 128 bits to store most of its values, which set the limits so high that they won't ever be encountered by anyone working in systems administration today. One directory can have 2^{48} files, of up to 16 exabytes each. A single pool can be up to 256 zettabytes, or 2^{78} bytes. A storage pool can contain up to 2^{64} devices, and a single host can have up to 2^{64} storage pools.

The good news is, we will not live long enough to hit these limits. The bad news is, we have all the expertise in migrating between filesystems. When technology hits ZFS' limits, those poor people won't be accustomed to migrating between filesystems. Fortunately, they'll have a few lingering ongoing FAT/UFS/extfs rollovers for practice.

Storage Pools

ZFS uses *storage pools* rather than disks. A storage pool is an abstraction atop the underlying storage providers, letting you separate the physical medium and the user-visible filesystem on top of it.

Use zpool(8) to view and manage a system's storage pools. Here's the pool from a default FreeBSD system.

```
# zpool status
  pool: zroot
 state: ONLINE
  scan: none requested
config:

   NAME            STATE   READ  WRITE  CKSUM
   zroot           ONLINE     0      0      0
     gpt/zfs0      ONLINE     0      0      0

errors: No known data errors
```

You get the pool's name and state first. Systems can have more than one ZFS pool—large systems, with dozens and dozens of hard drives, often have multiple pools. If this host had multiple storage pools, each would appear in a separate description like the sample above.

ZFS can perform many sorts of integrity checks on storage pools. The *scan* statement shows if any integrity check is being performed and the result of the most recent scan.

The last part of the pool list shows the layout of the virtual devices in the pool.

Virtual Devices

A storage pool contains one or more virtual devices, or *VDEVs*. A VDEV is similar to a traditional RAID device. A big RAID-5 presents itself to the filesystem layer as a single huge device, even though the sysadmin knows it's really a whole bunch of smaller disks. Virtual devices let you assign specific devices to specific roles. With VDEVs you can arrange the physical storage as needed.

The virtual device is where a whole bunch of ZFS' magic happens. A pool can be arranged for RAID-style redundancy. You can use providers as dedicated read and write caches, improving the virtual device's performance. Chapter 2 covers virtual devices in more depth.

ZFS' data redundancy and automated error correction also take place at the VDEV level. Everything in ZFS is checksummed for integrity verification. If your pool has sufficient redundancy, ZFS is self-healing. If your pool lacks redundancy, well, at least you know the data is damaged and you can (hopefully) restore from backup.[3]

The `zpool status` command that displays the health of a pool also shows the virtual devices in that pool. Look at the example in the previous section. This very simple pool, `zroot`, contains a single storage provider, `/dev/gpt/zfs0`. This provider is a GPT partition, not a disk. ZFS can use all sorts of underlying storage, as Chapter 2 discusses. Using a GPT partition is very common, but other options include whole disks, files, and any other GEOM provider. FreeBSD uses GEOM providers to support features such as encryption.

Blocks and Inodes

Traditional filesystems almost always use some variety of data block for storing data and maps the contents of those blocks with an index node. BSD's UFS and Linux's extfs call these *blocks* and *inodes*. Even Microsoft's FAT filesystems have data storage blocks and index nodes.

Like these filesystems, ZFS uses index blocks and data blocks. Unlike older filesystems, however, ZFS generates index nodes on demand. Whenever possible, ZFS creates storage blocks in sizes that fit the data. The variable sized blocks don't always fit every possible file you might create, but they're certainly more flexible than traditional filesystems.

---

3   ZFS does not eliminate the need for backups. The only thing that eliminates backups is absolute indifference.

Unlike UFS superblocks, dynamically generated index blocks can't be placed in known locations on the disk. How can ZFS cope with the possibility of damage to an index block? ZFS stores multiple copies of critical index blocks at algorithmically predictable locations. These *ditto blocks* get replicated in multiple locations on the disk. Chapter 3 discusses ZFS blocks, uberblocks, ditto blocks, transaction groups, and more.

Now that you know the bare basics of ZFS, the rest of this book merely fills in several hundred little details. We'll start at the very bottom of the stack, with the virtual devices.

Chapter 2: Virtual Devices

In this chapter we'll delve into how the sausage is made. This... is a pig—I mean, a disk. Disks are the physical manifestation of storage. Disks are evil. They lie about their characteristics and layout, they hide errors, and they fail in unexpected ways. ZFS means no longer having to fear that your disks are secretly plotting against you. Yes, your disks *are* plotting against you, but ZFS exposes their treachery and puts a stop to it.

To most effectively use the available disks with ZFS, you require a basic understanding of how the operating system presents disks to ZFS, and how ZFS arranges data on those disks.

Disks and Other Storage Media

ZFS can also run on storage media other than disks. Anything that is a FreeBSD GEOM storage provider can become a ZFS storage medium. ZFS even has support for using files as the backing storage, which is really great for testing but is not meant for production. ZFS can use any block device for its physical storage, but each type has its advantages and disadvantages.

Raw Disk Storage

Using an entire physical disk reduces complexity. Also, there is no partitioning to worry about, and no software or configuration between ZFS and the physical disk. However, the disadvantages usually outweigh these advantages.

Booting from a disk requires that the disk have a boot loader. A boot loader can only go on a partitioned disk. You cannot boot a raw disk. FreeBSD supports giving disks useful labels, but those labels live inside the partition information.

Worse, any replacement disks must be exactly the same size as the original disk, or larger. Not all 6 TB disks are the same size—disks from different vendors vary by a few megabytes. You don't care about these variances when setting up a system, but they're critical when replacing a disk. Most catalogs don't list the number of sectors in each disk, only the size, so finding a usable replacement can take several attempts. Replacing a drive that uses the traditional 512-byte sectors with one that uses 4096-byte (4K, also known as Advanced Format) sectors complicates things further. The original drive probably had a number of sectors not evenly divisible by 8. Thanks to the special math used by disk drives, the new drive might appear to be just a couple bytes smaller than the old drive even if it's a couple bytes larger.

Partition Storage

Instead of using an entire raw disk, you can partition a disk and then use one of the partitions for ZFS. The biggest advantage to this is that you can now boot from the disk that contains the ZFS partition, by creating a small boot partition, instead of requiring a separate boot device. Using partitions also allows you to use part of the disk space for other things, like a raw swap partition, another filesystem, or just leaving some wiggle room at the end of the disk so the replacement disk doesn't have to have a matching sector count. Partitioning also allows you to "short stroke" the drive to increase performance.

Many of the original Solaris ZFS administration guides recommend against using partitions (or, in Solaris terms, *slices*) for performance reasons. In Solaris, using a partition for a filesystem disables the write cache. In FreeBSD, disabling the write cache is completely separate from disk partitioning or filesystems. FreeBSD gives full performance when using ZFS on a partition.

FreeBSD supports a number of partitioning schemes, but GPT is strongly recommended. The older partitioning system, MBR, limited the number of primary partitions to four, while GPT supports up to 128 partitions. MBR can manage disks up to only 2 TB, while GPT can manage up to 8 ZB with 512 byte-sector disks and up to 64 ZB with 4 K-sector disks. *FreeBSD Mastery: Storage Essentials* covers FreeBSD's support for both partitioning methods.[4]

The disadvantage to using partitions is that you might lose some of the portability that ZFS provides. If you move disks from one system to another, the target system must be able to recognize the disk partitions.

GEOM Device Storage

ZFS can also use the various FreeBSD GEOM classes as its backing storage. These sit between the filesystem and the physical devices, and perform various functions. The GEOM classes provide features such as whole disk encryption (GELI, GBDE), high availability, labels, multipath, and pluggable schedulers. A GEOM class can be created based on an entire device, or on top of another GEOM class, such as a partition, multipath device, or encrypted disk.

GELI (the FreeBSD disk encryption subsystem) is the best way to achieve an encrypted ZFS pool. GELI encrypts and decrypts blocks as they are passed back and forth between ZFS and the physical disks, so it doesn't require ZFS to do anything different. GELI supports a number of different encryption algorithms, but the default AES-XTS offers

---

4   If you're storing your data on clay tablets, you may use bsdlabel(8) partitions.

the best performance, especially with a modern CPU that supports the AES New Instructions (AESNI). With the help of this hardware offload feature, GELI can encrypt data at over 1 GB/sec and decrypt even faster, meaning that adding encryption will not lower your performance, even on an SSD. GELI can also optionally provide data authentication (integrity verification), where it stores a Hashed Message Authentication Code (HMAC) with each sector. It uses this HMAC to verify the integrity (the data has not been tampered with), and authenticity (this data was written by you) of the data. If upon reading back the sector, the HMAC does not verify the data, an error is returned. The HMAC feature is not enabled by default, and is probably overkill for ZFS because ZFS provides its own checksumming on each data block.

High Availability Storage Technology (HAST) is FreeBSD's distributed storage solution. It allows you to mirror a block device between computers over the network. Using HAST as the backing storage for a ZFS pool allows you to mirror each backing disk to a second machine. The advantage to HAST is that it is real time; a block is not considered to be written until it has been written to all hosts in the HAST cluster. ZFS replication, on the other hand, is based on syncing periodic snapshots. However, with HAST the second machine cannot have the pool imported or mounted at the same time as the first machine. Compared to ZFS replication, where you can have the replicated pool active (but read-only) concurrently, HAST makes sense in only a few cases.

GEOM labels provide a handy way to attach a meaningful note to each disk or partition. There are many label types, including standards like disk ident, gptid, GPT labels, and the GEOM-specific glabel. Best practices for labeling drives appear in Chapter 0.

GEOM also supports multipath for high availability. Sometimes it is not just the disk that dies, but also the controller card, the backplane, or the cable. With multipath, enterprise drives that are "dual ported" can be connected to more than one HBA (a disk controller card without any RAID features). If each drive has a path to two different storage controllers, it can survive the loss of one of those controllers. However, when each disk is connected to two different controllers, the operating system sees each disk twice, once via each controller. The GEOM multipath class allows you to write a label to each disk, so that successive routes to the same disk are detected as such. This way you get one representation of each disk, backed by multiple paths to that disk via different controllers. We discuss multipath in *FreeBSD Mastery: Advanced ZFS*.

The GEOM scheduler module allows the administrator to specify different I/O scheduling algorithms in an attempt to achieve better performance. As of this writing, the currently available schedulers are "as," a simple form of anticipatory scheduling with only one queue, and "rr," anticipatory scheduling with round-robin service across each client queue. See `gsched(8)` for more details. The GEOM system makes it relatively easy to write additional scheduling modules for specific workloads.

File-Backed Storage

You can use a file-backed virtual disk as a ZFS storage device. While we certainly don't recommend this for production, file-backed disks can be useful for testing and experimenting.

Providers vs. Disks

"Provider" is a technical term in FreeBSD. A GEOM storage provider is a thing that offers data storage. It might be a disk. It might be a GEOM class that transforms the storage in some way. Technically speaking, this book should use the word provider instead of disk almost everywhere. You can use any GEOM provider as a back end for ZFS. The problem with this is, one physical disk can offer several different providers. Your pool might have several different providers, but if they're all on one disk, you've just shot your redundancy in the head.[5]

Where this book discusses "disks," we mean "some sort of provider on top of a disk." This disk doesn't have to be wholly dedicated to ZFS—you could have a swap partition and a ZFS partition on a disk and be perfectly fine. But you can't have two ZFS partitions on a single physical disk, mirror them, and have physical redundancy.

VDEVs: Virtual Devices

A virtual device, or VDEV, is the logical storage unit of ZFS. Each VDEV is composed of one or more GEOM providers. ZFS supports several different types of VDEV, which are differentiated by the type of redundancy the VDEV offers. The common mirrored disk, where each disk contains a copy of another disk, is one type of VDEV. Plain disks, with no redundancy, are another type of VDEV. And ZFS includes three different varieties of sophisticated RAID, called RAID-Z.

These VDEVs are arranged into the storage pools discussed in Chapter 3. Actual data goes on top of the pools, as Chapter 4 covers. But the arrangement of your virtual devices dictates how well the pool performs and how well it resists physical damage. Almost all of ZFS' redundancy comes from the virtual devices.

A storage pool consists of one or more VDEVs where the pool data is spread across those VDEVs with no redundancy. (You can add some redundancy with the `copies` property, as discussed in Chapter 4, but that provides no protection against total disk failure.) The ZFS pool treats VDEVs as single units that provide storage space. Storage pools cannot survive the loss of a VDEV, so it's important that you either use

---

5   FreeBSD's flexible storage system gives you the power to do stupid things. Don't.

VDEVs with redundancy or decide in advance that it's okay to lose the data in this pool.

Using multiple VDEVs in a pool creates systems similar to advanced RAID arrays. A RAID-Z2 array resembles RAID-6, but a ZFS pool with two RAID-Z2 VDEVs resembles RAID-60. Mirrored VDEVs look like RAID-1, but groups of them resemble RAID-10. In both of these cases, ZFS stripes the data across each VDEV with no redundancy. The individual VDEVs provide the redundancy.

VDEV Redundancy

A VDEV that contains more than one disk can use a number of different redundancy schemes to provide fault tolerance. Nothing can make a single disk sitting all by itself redundant. ZFS supports using mirrored disks and several parity-based arrays.

ZFS uses redundancy to self-heal. A VDEV without redundancy doesn't support self-healing. You can work around this at the dataset layer (with the `copies` property), but a redundant VDEV supports self-healing automatically.

Stripe (1 Provider)

A VDEV composed of a single disk is called a *stripe*, and has no redundancy. As you might expect, losing the single provider means that all data on the disk is gone. A stripe pool contains only single-disk VDEVs.

A ZFS pool stripes data across all the VDEVs in the pool and relies on the VDEV to provide redundancy. If one stripe device fails, the entire pool fails. All data stored on the pool is gone. This is fine for scratch partitions, but if you care about your data, use a type of VDEV that offers fault tolerance.

Mirrors (2+ Providers)

A mirror VDEV stores a complete copy of all data on every disk. You can lose all but one of the drives in the provider and still access your data. You can use any number of disks in a mirror.

Mirrors provide very good random and sequential read speeds because data can be read from all of the disks at once. Write performance suffers because all data must be written to all of the disks, and the operation is not complete until the slowest disk has finished.

RAID-Z1 (3+ Providers)

ZFS includes three modern RAID-style redundant VDEVs, called RAID-Z. RAID-Z resembles RAID-5, but includes checksumming to ensure file integrity. Between checksums and ZFS' copy-on-write features (Chapter 7), RAID-Z insures that incomplete writes do not result in an inconsistent filesystem.

RAID-Z spreads data and parity information across all of the disks. If a provider in the RAID-Z dies or starts giving corrupt data, RAID-Z uses the parity information to recalculate the missing data. You might hear that RAID-Z uses a provider to store parity information, but there's no single parity provider—the parity role is rotated through the providers, spreading the data.

A RAID-Z1 VDEV can withstand the failure of any single storage provider. If a second provider fails before the first failed drive is replaced, all data is lost. Rebuilding a disk array from parity data can take a long time. If you're using large disks—say, over 2 TB—there's a non-trivial chance of a second drive failing as you repair the first drive. For larger disks, you should probably look at RAID-Z2.

RAID-Z2 (4+ Providers)

RAID-Z2 resembles RAID-Z1, but has two parity disks per VDEV. Like RAID-6, RAID-Z2 allows it to continue to operate even with two failed providers. It is slightly slower than RAID-Z1, but allows you to be somewhat lazy in replacing your drives.

RAID-Z3 (5+ Providers)

The most paranoid form of RAID-Z, RAID-Z3 uses three parity disks per VDEV. Yes, you can have three failed disks in your five-disk array. It is slightly slower than RAID-Z2. Failure of a fourth disk results in total data loss.

RAID-Z Disk Configurations

One important thing to remember when using any version of RAID-Z is that the number of providers in a RAID-Z is completely fixed. You cannot add drives to a RAID-Z VDEV to expand them. You can expand the pool by adding VDEVs, but you cannot expand a VDEV by adding disks. There are no plans to add this feature.

Suppose you have a host that can accept 20 hard drives. You install 12 drives and use them as a single RAID-Z2, thinking that you will add more drives to your pool later as you need them. Those new drives will have to go in as separate RAID-Z2 VDEV.

What's more, your VDEVs will be unbalanced. Your pool will have a single 12-drive VDEV, and a second 8-drive VDEV. One will be slower than the other. ZFS will let you force it to pool these devices together, but it's a really bad idea to do so.

Plan ahead. Look at your physical gear, the number of drives you have to start with, and how you'll expand that storage. Our example server would be fine with on pool containing a single RAID-Z2 VDEV, and a completely separate pool containing the other eight disks in whatever arrangement you want. Don't cut your own throat before you even start!

The RAID-Z Rule of 2s

One commonly discussed configuration is to have a number of data disks equal to a multiple of two, plus the parity disks needed for a given RAID-Z level. That is, this rule says that a RAID-Z1 should use 2n+1 disks, or three, five, seven, nine, and so on. A RAID-Z2 should use 2n+2 disks (four, six, eight, and so on), while a RAID-Z3 should use 2n+3 (five, seven, nine, and so on).

This rule works—*if and only if* your data is composed of small blocks with a size that is a power of 2. Other factors make a much bigger difference, though. Compression is generally considered far more effective. Compressing your data reduces the size of the blocks, eliminating this benefit.

Repairing VDEVs

When a provider that belongs to a redundant VDEV fails, the VDEV it is a member of becomes "degraded." A degraded VDEV still has all of its data, but performance might be reduced. Chapter 5 covers replacing failed providers.

After the provider is replaced, the system must store data on the new provider. Mirrors make this easy: read the data from the remaining disk(s) and write it to the replacement. For RAID-Z, the data must be recalculated from parity.

The way that ZFS combines RAID and the filesystem means that ZFS knows which blocks contain data, and which blocks are free. Instead of having to write out every byte on to the new drive, ZFS needs to write only the blocks that are actually in use. A traditional RAID controller has no understanding or awareness of the filesystem layer, so it has no idea what is in use and what is free space. When a RAID controller replaces a disk, it must copy every byte of the new disk. This means a damaged ZFS RAID-Z heals much more quickly, reducing the chance of a concurrent failure that could cause data loss. We discuss ZFS recovery in Chapter 5.

RAID-Z versus traditional RAID

RAID-Z has a number of advantages compared to traditional RAID, but the biggest ones come from the fact that ZFS is the volume manager and the filesystem in addition to the disk redundancy layer.

Back in the day, filesystems could only work on one disk. If you had two disks, you needed two separate filesystems. Traditional RAID let you combine multiple disks into one virtual disk, permitting the creation of massive disks as large as 100 MB, or even bigger! Then the operating system puts its own filesystem on top of that, without any understanding of how the blocks will be laid out on the physical disks. At the same time, RAID could provide fault tolerance. Given the limitations of hardware and software at the time, RAID seemed a pretty good bet.

By combining the filesystem and the volume manager, ZFS can see exactly where all data lies and how the storage layer and the data interact. This allows ZFS to make a number of important decisions, such as ensuring that extra copies of important data such as ditto blocks (Chapter 3) are stored on separate disks. It does no good to have two or three copies of your critical data all on one underlying storage provider that can be wiped out by a single hardware failure. ZFS goes so far as to put the ditto blocks on adjacent disks, because it is statistically less likely that if two disks fail concurrently, they will be neighbors.

Traditional RAID can suffer from a shortcoming known as the "write hole," where two-step operations get cut short halfway through. RAID 5 and 6 devices chunk up data to be written to all of the data disks. Once this operation finishes, a parity block is calculated and stored on the parity disk. If the system crashes or the power is cut after the data is written but before the parity is written, the disk ends up in an indeterminate state. When the system comes back up, the data does not match the parity. The same thing can happen with mirrored drives if one drive finishes updating and the other does not.

Write hole problems are not noticed until you replace a failed disk. The incorrect parity or incorrect mirror results in the RAID device returning garbage data to the filesystem. Traditional filesystems return this garbage data as the contents of your file.

ZFS solves these problems with copy-on-write and checksums. Copy-on-write (Chapter 7) means data is never overwritten in place. Each update is transactional, and either completes fully or is not performed, returning the system to the state it was in before the update. ZFS also has checksums, so it can detect when a drive returns invalid data. When ZFS detects invalid data it replaces that data with the correct data from another source, such as additional copies of the data, mirrored drives, or RAID-Z parity. Combined, these create ZFS' self-healing properties.

Special VDEVs

Pools can use special-purpose VDEVs to improve the performance of the pool. These special VDEV types are not used to persistently store data, but instead temporarily hold additional copies of data on faster devices.

Separate Intent Log (SLOG, ZIL)

ZFS maintains a ZFS Intent Log (ZIL) as part of the pool. Similar to the journal in some other filesystems, this is where it writes in-progress operations, so they can be completed or rolled back in the event of a system crash or power failure. The ZIL is subject to the disk's normal operating conditions. The pool might have a sudden spike in use or latency related to load, resulting in slower performance.

One way to boost performance is to separate the ZIL from the normal pool operations. You can use a dedicated device as a Separate Intent Log, or SLOG, rather than using a regular part of the pool. The dedicated device is usually a small but very fast device, such as a very high-endurance SSD.

Rather than copying data from the SLOG to the pool's main storage in the order it's received, ZFS can batch the data in sensible groups and write it more efficiently.

Certain software insists on receiving confirmation that data it writes to disk is actually on the disk before it proceeds. Databases often do this to avoid corruption in the event of a system crash or power outage. Certain NFS operations do the same. By writing these requests to the faster log device and reporting "all done," ZFS accelerates these operations. The database completes the transaction and moves on. You get write performance almost at an SSD level, while using inexpensive disk as the storage media.

You can mirror your ZIL to prevent data loss.

Cache (L2ARC)

When a file is read from disk, the system keeps it in memory until the memory is needed for another purpose. This is old technology, used even back in the primordial BSD days. Look at `top(1)` on a UFS-based BSD system and you'll see a chunk of memory labeled Buf. That's the buffer cache.

The traditional buffer cache was designed decades ago, however. ZFS has an Adaptive Replacement Cache, or ARC, designed for modern hardware, that gives it more speed. The ARC retains the most recently and frequently accessed files.

Very few modern systems have enough RAM to cache as much as they want, however. Just as ZFS can use a SLOG to accelerate writes, it can use a very fast disk to accelerate reads. This is called a Level 2 ARC, or L2ARC.

When an object is used frequently enough to benefit from caching, but not frequently enough to rate being stored in RAM, ZFS can store it on a cache device. The L2ARC is typically a very fast and high-endurance SSD or NVMe device. Now, when that block of data is requested, it can be read from the faster SSD rather than the slower disks that make up the rest of the pool. ZFS knows which data has been changed on the back-end disk, so it can ensure that the read cache is synchronized with the data on the storage pool.

How VDEVs Affect Performance

Each different type of VDEV performs differently. Benchmarking and dissecting disk performance is a complex topic that would merit a great big textbook, if anyone would be bothered to read it. Any specific advice we were to give here would quickly become obsolete, so let's just discuss some general terms.

One common measurement is Input/Output Per Second or IOPS, the number of distinct operations the drive can perform each second. Spinning drive IOPS are usually physically limited by how quickly the read/write head can move from place to place over the platter. Solid state disks have such excellent performance because they don't need to physically move anything.

The number of non-parity spindles constrains streaming read and write performance of an undamaged pool. "Streaming" performance boils down to the number of megabytes per second (MB/s) the drive can read or write. When a drive reads or writes data sequentially, the heads do not have to seek back and forth to different locations. It is under these conditions that a drive will achieve its best possible streaming performance, giving the highest throughput. Spindle count affects both random and streaming performance. An array of 12 one-terabyte (12 x 1 TB) drives usually outperforms an array of six two-terabyte (6 x 2 TB) drives because the greater spindle and head counts increase both IOPS and streaming performance. Having more heads means that ZFS can be reading from, or writing to, more different locations on the disks at once, resulting in greater IOPS performance. More spindles mean more disks working as fast as they can to read and write your data. The greater number of drives require a larger shelf or chassis, more power, and more controllers, however.

Other common measurements include read bandwidth, write bandwidth, space efficiency, and streaming performance.

Generally speaking, mirrors can provide better IOPS and read bandwidth, but RAID-Z can provide better write bandwidth and much better space efficiency.

A pool with multiple VDEVs stripes its data across all the VDEVs. This increases performance but might cost space, as each individual VDEV has its own redundant disks. A pool with multiple VDEVs probably has increased reliability and fault tolerance. While ZFS' redundancy is all at the VDEV level, a pool with multiple redundant VDEVs can probably withstand more disk failures. The more VDEVs you have in a pool, the better the pool performs.

Let's go through some common VDEV configurations and see how the various possible arrangements affect performance and capacity. Assume we're using a set of modest commodity 1 TB spinning disks. Each disk is capable of 250 IOPS and streaming read/writes at 100 MB/s.

One Disk

With only one disk, there is only one possible configuration, a single ZFS stripe VDEV. This is the most basic configuration, and provides no fault tolerance. If that one disk dies, all of your data is gone.

Table 1: Single Disk Virtual Device Configurations

Config	Read IOPS	Write IOPS	Read MB/s	Write MB/s	Usable Space	Fault Tolerance
Stripe	250	250	100	100	1 TB (100%)	none

The performance characteristics of a one-disk stripe device look suspiciously like the characteristics of the underlying disk. Weird, huh?

Two Disks

If your system has two disks, you can build your pool out of two stripe VDEVs or a single mirror VDEV.

Striped VDEVs double the available storage and bandwidth, but also double the risk of failure. ZFS spreads the blocks of each file over the two disks. If either disk fails, all of the data is unusable.

Using a single mirrored VDEV stores each block of data on both disks. This maintains the improved read performance, as blocks can be read from both disks at once. But you get only the capacity of the smallest disk. Write performance is limited to the speed of the slowest disk. One disk can fail, however, and the pool will still be usable.

Table 2: Two-Disk Virtual Device Configurations

Config	Read IOPS	Write IOPS	Read MB/s	Write MB/s	Usable Space	Fault Tolerance
2 x Stripe	500	500	200	200	2 TB (100%)	none
1 x 2 disk Mirror	500	250	200	100	1 TB (50%)	1

As the table shows, our mirror pool gets half the write performance of the striped pool and has half the space.

Three Disks

Three disks means more options, including a deeper mirror and RAID-Z. You could also use a pool of three stripe disks, but the odds of failure are much higher.

A deeper mirror has more disks, providing more fault tolerance and improved read performance. More spindles and heads mean that the VDEV can read data from the least busy of the three drives, serving random reads more quickly. Write performance in a mirror is still limited to the slowest of the drives in the mirror.

RAID-Z1 offers better space efficiency, as the fault tolerance requires only one of the disks in the VDEV. Data is spread across all of the drives, so they must work together to perform reads and writes. Spreading the data across all the drives improves streaming write performance. Unlike a mirror, in RAID-Z all drives can write their share of data simultaneously, instead of each drive writing identical data.

Table 3: Three-Disk Virtual Device Configurations

Config	Read IOPS	Write IOPS	Read MB/s	Write MB/s	Usable Space	Fault Tolerance
1 x 3 disk Mirror	750	250	300	100	1 TB (33%)	2
1 x 3 disk RAID-Z1	250	250	200	200	2 TB (66%)	1

Note here that IOPS don't necessarily scale to actual read/write performance. A mirror VDEV has three times the read IOPS of a RAID-Z1 because the head in each drive can work independently, whereas in RAID-Z the heads must work together. In megabytes per second mirrors have the advantage of using all of their disks' throughput for data, whereas RAID-Z1 loses one disk's worth of throughput because of the parity data. A three-disk mirror also writes half as many

MB/s because it writes the same data to every disk, whereas RAID-Z1 can spread the writes out over all the disks but loses some throughput to parity.

Four or Five Disks

With four or five disks, you get even more options.

Multiple mirror VDEVs (similar to traditional RAID 10) provide the best possible performance for random I/O workloads like databases. When you divide four disks into two mirror VDEVs of two disks each, ZFS stripes the writes across both mirrors. One mirror holds half of your data, and the other mirror the other half. This helps mitigate the write bottleneck of mirrors, while still providing the impressive read performance.

With four disks, RAID-Z2 becomes an option. RAID-Z2's two parity disks mean that the VDEV can continue to operate with the loss of any two disks. When compared to a mirror with the same number of disks, the performance is worse; however, it no longer matters which two disks fail concurrently.

At five disks, we can deploy RAID-Z3. A RAID-Z3 VDEV can survive the loss of any three disks. A RAID-Z3 exchanges performance for fault tolerance.

And RAID-Z1 remains an option, of course.

Table 4: Four- or Five-Disk Virtual Device Configurations

Disks	Config	Read IOPS	Write IOPS	Read MB/s	Write MB/s	Usable Space	Fault Tolerance
4	2 x 2 disk Mirror	1000	500	400	200	2 TB (50%)	2 (1/VDEV)
4	1 x 4 disk RAID-Z1	250	250	300	300	3 TB (75%)	1
4	1 x 4 disk RAID-Z2	250	250	200	200	2 TB (50%)	2
5	1 x 5 disk RAID-Z1	250	250	400	400	4 TB (80%)	1
5	1 x 5 disk RAID-Z2	250	250	300	300	3 TB (60%)	2
5	1 x 5 disk RAID-Z3	250	250	200	200	2 TB (40%)	3

Note how the streaming (MB/s) read and write performance of RAID-Z1 compares with RAID-Z2, and how the performance of RAID-Z3 compares to both. Adding a parity disk means sacrificing that disk's throughput.

The fault tolerance of multiple mirror VDEVs is slightly tricky. Remember, redundancy is per-VDEV, not per pool. Each mirror VDEV still provides n - 1 fault tolerance. As long as one drive in each mirror VDEV still works, all data is accessible. With two two-disk mirror VDEVs in your pool, you can lose one disk from each VDEV and keep running. If you lose two disks from the same VDEV, however, the pool dies and all data is lost.

Six to Twelve Disks

With large numbers of disks, the decision shifts to balancing fault tolerance, space efficiency, and performance.

Six disks could become three two-disk mirror VDEVs, giving you a fair amount of space and good write performance. You could opt for a pair of three-disk mirror VDEVs, giving you less space, but allowing two disks out of each set of three to fail without risking data loss. Or they could become a RAID-Z VDEV.

Get many more than six disks and you can have multiple RAID-Z VDEVs in a pool. A dozen disks can be operated together as a single VDEV giving the most available space, or can be split into two separate VDEVs, providing less usable space but better performance and more fault tolerance.

Table 5: Six- to Twelve-Disk Virtual Device Configurations

Disks	Config	Read IOPS	Write IOPS	Read MB/s	Write MB/s	Usable Space	Fault Tolerance
6	3 x 2 disk Mirror	1500	750	600	300	3 TB (50%)	3 (1/VDEV)
6	2 x 3 disk Mirror	1500	500	600	200	2 TB (33%)	4 (2/VDEV)
6	1 x 6 disk RAID-Z1	250	250	500	500	5 TB (83%)	1
6	1 x 6 disk RAID-Z2	250	250	400	400	4 TB (66%)	2
6	1 x 6 disk RAID-Z3	250	250	300	300	3 TB (50%)	3
12	6 x 2 disk Mirror	3000	1500	1200	600	6 TB (50%)	6 (1/VDEV)
12	4 x 3 disk Mirror	3000	1000	1200	400	4 TB (33%)	8 (2/VDEV)
12	1 x 12 disk RAID-Z1	250	250	1100	1100	11 TB (92%)	1
12	2 x 6 disk RAID-Z1	500	500	1000	1000	10 TB (83%)	2 (1/VDEV)
12	3 x 4 disk RAID-Z1	750	750	900	900	9 TB (75%)	3 (1/VDEV)
12	1 x 12-disk RAID-Z2	250	250	1000	1000	10 TB (83%)	2
12	2 x 6-disk RAID-Z2	500	500	800	800	8 TB (66%)	4 (2/VDEV)
12	1 x 12-disk RAID-Z3	250	250	900	900	9 TB (75%)	3
12	2 x 6-disk RAID-Z3	500	500	600	600	6TB (50%)	6 (3/VDEV)

Using multiple RAID-Z devices in a pool is much like using multiple mirror devices in a pool. Tolerance to disk failures is per-VDEV, not per pool. Your 12-disk array of two six-disk RAID-Z2 VDEVs can handle the loss of four disks, provided you lose only two disks per VDEV.

Many Disks

Common advice is to use no more than nine to 12 disks per VDEV. You can use more, but ZFS isn't designed for that. Let's look at an array of 36 disks to see some possible arrangements and their performance impact.

Table 6: 36-Disk Virtual Device Configurations

Config	Read IOPS	Write IOPS	Read MB/s	Write MB/s	Usable Space	Fault Tolerance
18 x 2 disk Mirror	9000	4500	3600	1800	18 TB (50%)	18 (1/VDEV)
12 x 3 disk Mirror	9000	3000	3600	1200	12 TB (33%)	24 (2/VDEV)
1 x 36 disk RAID-Z2	250	250	3400	3400	34 TB (94%)	2
2 x 18 disk RAID-Z2	500	500	3200	3200	32 TB (89%)	4 (2/VDEV)
4 x 9 disk RAID-Z2	1000	1000	2800	2800	28 TB (78%)	8 (2/VDEV)
6 x 6 disk RAID-Z2	1500	1500	2400	2400	24 TB (66%)	12 (2/VDEV)

By using more VDEVs, you can create screaming fast pools. A pool of 18 two-disk mirror VDEVs can read data more quickly than most anything else—and it can lose 18 drives before failing! Yes, they have to be the right 18 drives, but if you have two disk shelves with different power supplies, that's entirely possible. On the other hand, if the wrong two disks in that pool fail, your entire pool dies.

Adding parity or mirrors to each VDEV increases reliability. A greater number of VDEVs increases performance. Your job is to juggle these two characteristics to support your environment.

Each VDEV is limited to the random read/write performance of the slowest disk, so if you have too many disks in one VDEV, you are surrendering performance for only a small gain in space efficiency. While you can add L2ARC and SLOG devices to improve performance, it's best to avoid these problems altogether.

So if more VDEVs are always better, why is the 6 x 6 disk RAID-Z2 pool so much slower at reading and writing compared to the 1 x 36 disk RAID-Z2 pool? The answer lies in the fault tolerance column. When you have more RAID-Z2 VDEVs, you have more redundancy, and you can survive more failures. When a disk is providing fault tolerance, it is storing an extra copy of your data, so it can replace a copy that is lost when a disk fails. The system recalculates and stores parity data every time the data changes. Parity data isn't used when reading files unless the original copy is missing. The disks used for parity no longer contribute to streaming performance. You can restore that performance by adding more disks. A 6 x 8 disk RAID-Z2 pool would have the equivalent of 36 data disks and 12 parity disks, and be able to outperform the 1 x 36 disk RAID-Z2 pool.

Let's take what you know about VDEVs, and create some actual pools with them.

Chapter 3: Pools

ZFS pools, or *zpools*, form the middle of the ZFS stack, connecting the lower-level virtual devices to the user-visible filesystem. Pools are where many filesystem-level tasks happen, such as allocating blocks of storage. At the ZFS pool level you can increase the amount of space available to your ZFS dataset, or add special virtual devices to improve reading or writing performance.

ZFS Blocks

Traditional filesystems such as UFS and extfs place data on the disk in fixed-size blocks. The filesystem has special blocks, called *inodes*, that index which blocks belong to which files. Even non-Unix filesystems like NTFS and FAT use similar structures. It's a standard across the industry.

ZFS does not pre-configure special index blocks. It only uses storage blocks, also known as stripes. Each block contains index information to link the block to other blocks on the disk in a tree. ZFS computes hashes of all information in the block and stores the information in the block and in the parent block. Each block is a complete unit in and of itself. A file might be partially missing, but what exists is coherent.

Not having dedicated special index blocks sounds great, but surely ZFS needs to start somewhere! Every data tree needs a root. ZFS uses

45

a special block called an *uberblock* to store a pointer to the filesystem root. ZFS never changes data on the disk—rather, when a block changes, it writes a whole new copy of the block with the modified data. (We discuss this copy-on-write behavior in depth in Chapter 6.) A data pool reserves 128 blocks for uberblocks, used in sequence as the underlying pool changes. When the last uberblock gets used, ZFS loops back to the beginning.

The uberblocks are not the only critical blocks. ZFS copies blocks containing vital information like filesystem metadata and pool data into multiple *ditto blocks*. If a main block is damaged, ZFS checks the ditto block for a backup copy. Ditto blocks are stored as far as possible from each other, either on separate disks or on separate parts of a single disk. (ZFS has no special ability to see the layout of the disk hardware, but it makes a valiant guess.)

ZFS commits changes to the storage media in *transaction groups*, or *txg*. Transaction groups contain several batched changes, and have an incrementing 64-bit number. Each transaction group uses the next uberblock in line. ZFS identifies the most current uberblock out of the group of 128 by looking for the uberblock with the highest transaction number.

ZFS does use some blocks for indexing, but these znodes and dnodes can use any storage block in the pool. They aren't like UFS2 or extfs index nodes, assigned when creating the filesystem.

Stripes, RAID, and Pools

You've certainly heard the word *stripe* in connection with storage, probably many times. A ZFS pool "stripes" data across the virtual devices. A traditional RAID "stripes" data across the physical devices. What is a stripe, and how does it play into a pool?

A stripe is a chunk of data that's written to a single device. Most traditional RAID uses a 128 KB stripe size. When you're writing a file to a traditional RAID device, the RAID software writes to each drive in 128 KB chunks, usually in parallel. Similarly, reads from a traditional RAID array take place in increments of the stripe size. While you can customize the stripe size to fit a server's workload, the hardware's capacity and the software's limitations greatly restrict stripe size.

Stripes do not provide any redundancy. Traditional RAID gets its redundancy from parity and/or mirroring. ZFS pools get any redundancy from the underlying VDEVs.

ZFS puts stripes on rocket-driven roller skates. A ZFS dataset uses a default stripe size of 128 KB, but ZFS is smart enough to dynamically change that stripe size to fit the equipment and the workload. If a 32 KB stripe size makes sense for a particular chunk of data, but 64 KB makes sense for another piece of data, ZFS uses the appropriate size for each one. The ZFS developers have completed support for stripe sizes up to 1 MB. This feature is already available in FreeBSD-CURRENT, and is expected to be included in FreeBSD 10.2 and later.

A ZFS pool has much more flexibility than a traditional RAID. Traditional RAID has a fixed and inflexible data layout (although some hardware vendors have their own proprietary RAID systems with more flexibility). The RAID software writes to each disk in a deterministic order. ZFS has more flexibility. If you have a five-disk traditional RAID array, that array will always have five disks. You cannot change the array by adding disks. While you might be able to exchange the disks for larger disks, doing so won't change the array's size. Creating a RAID device petrifies the array's basic characteristics.

ZFS pools not only tolerate changes, but they're designed to easily accept additions as well. If you have a ZFS pool with five VDEVs and you want to add a sixth, that's fine. ZFS accepts that VDEV and starts striping data on that device without blinking. You cannot add storage to RAID-Z VDEVs, only VDEVs to pools. The number of providers in a RAID-Z VDEV is fixed at creation time.

With ZFS, though, that virtual device can be any type of VDEV ZFS supports. Take two VDEVs that are mirror pairs. Put them in a single zpool. ZFS stripes data across them. In traditional RAID, a stripe on top of mirrors would be called RAID-10. For most use cases, RAID-10 is the highest-performance RAID you can have. Where traditional RAID-10 has a fixed size, however, you can add additional VDEVs to a pool. Expanding your RAID-10 means backing up your data, adding disks to the RAID array, and restoring the data. Expanding your zpool means adding more VDEVs to the pool. RAID-10 also allows a depth of up to two disks, where ZFS allows a depth of up to 2^{64}.

Remember, though, that pools do not provide any redundancy. All ZFS redundancy comes from the underlying VDEVs.

Viewing Pools

To see all of the pools on your system, run zpool list.

```
# zpool list
NAME    SIZE   ALLOC  FREE   EXPANDSZ  FRAG  CAP  DEDUP  HEALTH  ALTROOT
db      2.72T  1.16G  2.72T    -        0%   0%   1.00x  ONLINE  -
zroot   920G   17.3G  903G     -        2%   1%   1.00x  ONLINE  -
```

The first column gives the pool name. This system has two pools, db and zroot.

The next three columns give size and usage information on each pool. You'll get the size, the amount of space used, and the amount of free space.

The EXPANDSZ column shows if the underlying storage providers have any free space. You might be able to expand the amount of space in this pool, as discussed in Chapter 5. This space includes blocks that will go to parity information, so expanding the pool won't give you this much usable space.

Under FRAG you'll see the amount of fragmentation in this pool. Fragmentation degrades filesystem performance.

The CAP column shows what percentage of the available space is used.

The DEDUP entry shows the amount of deduplication that's happened on the filesystem. Chapter 6 covers deduplication.

The pool's HEALTH column reflects the status of the underlying VDEVs. If a storage provider fails, your first hint will be any status other than ONLINE. Chapter 5 discusses pool health.

Finally, the ALTROOT shows where this pool is mounted, or its "alternate root." Chapter 4 covers alternate roots.

If you want to know the information for a specific pool or pools, list the pool names after `zpool list`. This shows only the output of the storage pools prod and test.

```
# zpool list prod test
```

If you want more detailed information on your pools, including the utilization of underlying drives, add the `-v` option. You must give the option before any pool name.

```
# zpool list -v zroot
```

The `-p` flag prints numbers in bytes rather than the more human-friendly format, and `-H` eliminates the column headers. These options are useful for automation and management scripts.

For a more detailed view of a system's pools, including the underlying VDEV layout, use `zpool status`. We'll see lots of examples of `zpool status` when we create pools.

To briefly check your pools, run `zpool status -x`.

```
# zpool status -x
all pools are healthy
```

Sometimes, that's all you need.

Multiple VDEVs

A pool can include multiple VDEVs. Adding VDEVs not only increases the space available in the pool but also increases the performance. A pool splits all writes between the VDEVs. A small file might need only a single stripe, which would go on a single VDEV, but if you're writing a whole bunch of small files ZFS divides the writes between the VDEVs.

Chapter 2 talks about the performance of various VDEV types. That performance percolates up into the pool level. If you're reading a large file from across multiple VDEVs, the file read finishes once the last (usually the slowest) drive finishes calling up its part of the data. If your pool includes multiple VDEVs, however, that slowest drive contains only a fraction of the file, somewhat reducing the time needed to access it. Remember, the slowest part of reading data from a storage provider is seeking the head to the correct piece of disk to call it from, so it's not as simple as dividing the time by the number of VDEVs— but additional VDEVs in a pool do improve performance.

Best practices call for using only identical storage VDEVs in a pool. If you have a bunch of mirrored VDEVs in your pool, don't go adding a RAID-Z3 device to the pool. Mixed storage VDEVs foul up pool performance terribly and make ZFS work harder as it optimally spreads the data between the devices. You *can* do this, but you shouldn't.[6]

---

6   ZFS follows the Unix tradition of not preventing you from doing daft things, because that would also prevent you from doing clever things.

Removing VDEVs

You cannot currently remove a VDEV from a pool. Each VDEV has data on it. You can remove disks from certain types of VDEV, but the VDEV as a whole has critical pool data on it. For example, you can remove a disk from a mirror VDEV, but you cannot remove the entire VDEV from the pool. Normally you'd remove a disk from a VDEV only when it fails. Forcibly removing a VDEV from a pool—say, by pulling the storage providers—destroys the pool. The ability to remove a VDEV from a stripe or mirror pool is expected to arrive in OpenZFS in late 2015, but it's not yet possible. Support for removing RAID-Z devices is on the road map, but work has not yet started.

This means you cannot shrink a pool. If you want to make a pool smaller, you must move the data on that pool to a new, smaller pool and then recycle the disks from the original pool.

Pools Alignment and Disk Sector Size

ZFS expects to have an in-depth knowledge of the storage medium, including the sector size of the underlying providers. If your pools don't use the correct sector size, or if ZFS' sectors don't align to the physical sectors on the disk, your storage performance will drop by half or more. These are orthogonal problems, but failing to plan for either one will crush your system.

We'll discuss partition alignment and ZFS sector size separately.

Partition Alignment

Disks report their sector size, so this isn't a problem—except when it is. Many disks report that they have 512-byte sectors, but they really have 4096-byte (4K) sectors. *FreeBSD Mastery: Storage Essentials* discusses this in depth, so we won't go through this in painful detail here.

Older partition management schemes, like the venerable Master Boot Record (MBR), included all sorts of hairy math to make sure that disk partitions conformed to the disk's physical characteristics. Modern partition schemes like GUID Partition Tables (GPT) know that physical disks speak with forked tongue and that those old MBR-based restrictions are utterly bogus, and so require only that partitions fill complete sectors.

But when a disk lies about its sector size, gpart(8) lets you create partitions that begin or end halfway through a physical sector. Each read or write to the disk requires touching two physical sectors. This wreaks havoc on performance.

Certain SSDs also expect partitions to be aligned along 128 KB or 1 MB boundaries.

The easy way to avoid alignment problems is to make all GPT partitions begin and end on megabyte boundaries. Add the -a 1m argument to your gpart add commands.

ZFS Sector Size

ZFS defaults to assuming a 512-byte sector size. Using a 512-byte filesystem sector size on a disk with physical 512-byte sectors is perfectly fine. Using a 512-byte filesystem sector on a 4K-sector disk makes the hardware work harder. Assume you want to write 4 KB of data on such a disk. Rather than telling the hard drive to write a single physical sector, the hard drive is told to modify the first eighth of the sector, then the second eighth, then the third, and so on. Doing a 512-byte write to a 4 KB sector means reading the entire 4 KB, modifying the small section, then writing it back. This is much slower than just overwriting the entire sector. Your performance plummets. If ZFS uses a 4K sector size on a disk with 512-byte sectors, the disk hardware breaks up the access requests into physical sector sizes, at very little performance cost.

While using a larger sector size does not impact performance, it does reduce space efficiency when you're storing many small files. If you have a whole bunch of 1 KB files, each occupies a single sector.

ZFS sector size is a property of each virtual device in a pool. You cannot change a virtual device's sector size, even when exporting the pool or replacing a failed drive.

Combined, these two facts mean that it's almost always preferable to force ZFS to use 4K sectors, regardless of the sector size reported by the underlying disk. Using the larger ZFS sector size won't hurt performance except on certain specific database operations, and even then only when using disks that really and for true use 512-byte sectors.

ZFS uses the sector size of the device that reports the largest sector size. If all of your devices claim to use 512-byte sectors, and you don't set a larger sector size, a virtual device built out of those devices will use 512-byte sectors. Including a single device with 4096-byte sectors in your VDEV forces ZFS to use 4096-byte sectors.

Don't trust that your 4K-sector devices report their sector size. Tell ZFS to insist on always using 4K sectors.

A pool variable called the *ashift* controls sector size. An ashift of 9 tells ZFS to use 512-byte sectors. An ashift of 12 tells ZFS to use 4096-byte sectors. (Why 9 and 12? 2^9 is 512, while 2^{12} is 4096.)[7] The way you set ashift depends on your FreeBSD release.

FreeBSD 10.1 and Newer Ashift

Set the system's default ashift with the sysctl vfs.zfs.min_auto_ashift, either in */etc/sysctl.conf* or at the command line.

```
# sysctl vfs.zfs.min_auto_ashift=12
```

---

7   Because *everyone* sees "9" and thinks 2^9, don't they?

Use the command line during installation, but also set it permanently in /etc/sysctl.conf so you don't forget when creating new pools.

This book's examples assume that you're using FreeBSD 10.1 or newer. For older FreeBSD versions, you'll need to set the ashift each time rather than setting the sysctl.

Older FreeBSD Ashift

FreeBSD versions older than 10.1 lack the ashift sysctl found in newer FreeBSD versions, so you have to rely on ZFS' internal sector-size-detection code. This code reads the sector size from the underlying storage medium—namely, the storage provider.

This case highlights the critical difference between a provider and a disk. FreeBSD lets you create a pass-through device with the GEOM module gnop(8). The gnop module lets you insert arbitrary data between your storage devices—in this case, enforcing a sector size. You create a gnop device that says, "Pass everything through transparently, but insist on a 4096-byte sector size." Use that device to create your zpool. Here, we add a gnop device to the partition labeled /dev/gpt/zfs0.

```
# gnop create -S 4096 /dev/gpt/zfs0
```

This creates the device /dev/gpt/zfs0.nop. Use this provider as one member of the VDEV, and ZFS will pick up on the sector size for that VDEV. The rest of this chapter discusses creating various ZFS pools, but here's an example of using this device when creating a mirrored pool.

```
# zpool create compost mirror gpt/zfs0.nop gpt/zfs1
```

Providers created with gnop(8) are temporary, disappearing at reboot. As gnop(8) passes everything through to the device, though, ZFS will find metadata on the underlying device. ZFS will no longer try to detect the disk's sector size, as it has already set its sector size.

Creating Pools and VDEVs

Create pools and virtual devices simultaneously with `zpool(8)`. You'll also use `zpool(8)` to add VDEVs to an existing pool and swap out failed devices, but we'll cover all that in Chapter 5. Here we'll create striped pools, mirrors, and pools on each of the RAID-Z devices. Chapter 2 discusses each VDEV type.

You need to set the ashift only once before creating as many pools as you like. You don't have to reset it each time you create a pool. We expect most readers to skip through this book until they find the entry for the type of pool they create, though, so we listed "set ashift" in all of them.

Sample Drives

Chapter 0 recommends labeling drives by physical location and serial number, so you can easily identify failed hardware. For production, that's very useful. For a book, however, longer device names make comprehension more difficult. Our examples use GPT labels of *zfs* and a number. This chapter uses six 1 TB drives, each with a 1 GB swap partition and a large ZFS partition, created with gpart(8).

```
# gpart create -s gpt da0
# gpart add -a 1m -s1g -l sw0 -t freebsd-swap da0
# gpart add -a 1m -l zfs0 -t freebsd-zfs da0
```

The resulting disk has the following partitions.

```
# gpart show -l da0
=>        40  1953525088  da0  GPT  (932G)
          40        2008    -  free -  (1.0M)
        2048     2097152    1  sw0  (1.0G)
     2099200  1951424512    2  zfs0  (931G)
  1953523712        1416    -  free -  (708K)
```

We manage the ZFS pools with the GPT labels, so the examples reference *gpt/zfs0* through *gpt/zfs5*. In production, use meaningful labels that map disks to physical locations.

Striped Pools

Some storage pools don't need redundancy, but do need lots of space. Scratch partitions for engineering and physics computations are common use cases for this kind of storage. Use `zpool create`, the pool name, and list the devices in the pool. Remember to set the ashift before creating the pool.

Here we create a pool of five storage providers.

```
# sysctl vfs.zfs.min_auto_ashift=12
# zpool create compost gpt/zfs0 gpt/zfs1 gpt/zfs2 \
  gpt/zfs3 gpt/zfs4
```

If the command succeeds, you get no output back. See if the pool exists with `zpool status`.

```
# zpool status
  pool: compost
 state: ONLINE
  scan: none requested
config:

NAME           STATE   READ   WRITE   CKSUM
compost        ONLINE     0       0       0
  gpt/zfs0     ONLINE     0       0       0
  gpt/zfs1     ONLINE     0       0       0
  gpt/zfs2     ONLINE     0       0       0
  gpt/zfs3     ONLINE     0       0       0
  gpt/zfs4     ONLINE     0       0       0
```

All five providers appear. Each provider is its own VDEV. This is a big pool for a system this size.

This pool stripes data across all the member VDEVs, but the VDEVs have no redundancy. Most real-world applications require redundancy. The simplest sort of redundancy is the mirror.

Mirrored Pools

Mirrored devices copy all data to multiple storage providers. If any one provider on the mirror fails, the pool still has another copy of the data. Traditional mirrors have two disks, although more is certainly possible.

Use the same `zpool create` command and the pool name. Before listing the storage devices, use the `mirror` keyword. Set the system ashift before creating the pool.

```
# sysctl vfs.zfs.min_auto_ashift=12
# zpool create reflect mirror gpt/zfs0 gpt/zfs1
```

Check the pool's configuration with `zpool status`.

```
# zpool status
  pool: reflect
 state: ONLINE
  scan: none requested
config:

NAME            STATE   READ  WRITE  CKSUM
reflect         ONLINE   0      0      0
  mirror-0      ONLINE   0      0      0
    gpt/zfs0    ONLINE   0      0      0
    gpt/zfs1    ONLINE   0      0      0

errors: No known data errors
```

The `zpool` command created a new layer here, something called *mirror-0*. The mirror-0 entry is a VDEV. This VDEV contains two devices, *gpt/zfs0* and *gpt/zfs1*.

You can certainly have a mirror with many disks if this fits your needs. Too many copies are better than not enough.

```
# zpool create reflect mirror gpt/zfs0 gpt/zfs1 \
    gpt/zfs2 gpt/zfs3
```

This might be an example of going too far, however (although we do discuss splitting a mirror into multiple pools in *FreeBSD Mastery: Advanced ZFS*.)

RAID-Z Pools

The redundancy you get from mirrors is fast and reliable, but not terribly complicated or exciting. RAID-Z offers greater flexibility at a complexity cost, which makes it more exciting.[8] Create a RAID-Z pool much as you would any other zpool: run `zpool create` and give the pool name, the type, and the storage devices. Here we create a RAID-Z (or RAID-Z1) pool.

```
# sysctl vfs.zfs.min_auto_ashift=12
# zpool create bucket raidz1 gpt/zfs0 gpt/zfs1 gpt/zfs2
```

The new pool's status shows a new VDEV, called *raidz1-0*, with three providers.

```
# zpool status bucket
  pool: bucket
 state: ONLINE
  scan: none requested
config:

NAME            STATE    READ    WRITE    CKSUM
bucket          ONLINE    0        0        0
  raidz1-0      ONLINE    0        0        0
    gpt/zfs0    ONLINE    0        0        0
    gpt/zfs1    ONLINE    0        0        0
    gpt/zfs2    ONLINE    0        0        0
```

If any one disk in this pool fails, the data remains intact. Other RAID-Z levels have even more redundancy. Here we pull six providers into a RAID-Z3. The only difference between creating the RAID-Z3 and the RAID-Z1 is the use of `raidz3` and the additional devices needed.

```
# zpool create bucket raidz3 gpt/zfs0 gpt/zfs1 \
    gpt/zfs2 gpt/zfs3 gpt/zfs4 gpt/zfs5
```

As you might guess by now, the pool's status shows a new device called *raidz3-0*.

---

8   *Exciting* is a bad word in systems administration.

```
# zpool status
  pool: bucket
 state: ONLINE
  scan: none requested
config:

NAME             STATE   READ WRITE  CKSUM
bucket           ONLINE     0     0      0
  raidz3-0       ONLINE     0     0      0
    gpt/zfs0     ONLINE     0     0      0
    gpt/zfs1     ONLINE     0     0      0
  ...
```

All of these pools have a single VDEV. What if you want multiple
VDEVs, though?

Multi-VDEV Pools

You can create a pool with multiple VDEVs. The keywords *mirror*,
raidz, *raidz2*, and *raidz3* all tell zpool(8) to create a new VDEV. Any
storage providers listed after one of those keywords goes into creating a new instance of that VDEV. When one of the keywords appears
again, zpool(8) starts with a new VDEV.

The opening of this chapter covered striping across multiple mirrors, simulating a traditional RAID-10 setup. Here we do exactly that.

```
# sysctl vfs.zfs.min_auto_ashift=12
# zpool create barrel mirror gpt/zfs0 gpt/zfs1 \
    mirror gpt/zfs2 gpt/zfs3
```

The first three words, zpool create barrel, tell zpool(8) to in-
stantiate a new pool, named *barrel*. The mirror keyword says "create a
mirror." We then have two storage providers, *gpt/zfs0* and *gpt/zfs1*.
These storage providers go into the first mirror. The word mirror appears again, telling zpool(8) that the previous VDEV is complete and
we're starting on a new VDEV. The second VDEV also has two storage
providers, *gpt/zfs2* and *gpt/zfs3*. This pool's status looks different
than anything we've seen before.

```
# zpool status barrel
  pool: barrel
 state: ONLINE
  scan: none requested
config:

NAME            STATE   READ  WRITE  CKSUM
barrel          ONLINE    0      0      0
 mirror-0       ONLINE    0      0      0
  gpt/zfs0      ONLINE    0      0      0
  gpt/zfs1      ONLINE    0      0      0
 mirror-1       ONLINE    0      0      0
  gpt/zfs2      ONLINE    0      0      0
  gpt/zfs3      ONLINE    0      0      0
```

The pool has two VDEVs, mirror-0 and mirror-1. Each VDEV includes two storage devices. We know that ZFS stripes data across all the VDEVs. Stripes over mirrors are RAID-10.

You can also arrange multi-VDEV pools in ways that have no common RAID equivalent. While software RAID systems like some of FreeBSD's GEOM classes would let you build similar RAIDs, you won't find them on a hardware RAID card. Here we create a pool that stripes data across two RAID-Z1 VDEVs.

```
# zpool create vat raidz1 gpt/zfs0 gpt/zfs1 gpt/zfs2 \
    raidz1 gpt/zfs3 gpt/zfs4 gpt/zfs5
```

The first RAID-Z1 VDEV includes three storage providers, *gpt/zfs0*, *gpt/zfs1*, and *gpt/zfs2*. The second includes *gpt/zfs3*, *gpt/zfs4*, and *gpt/zfs5*. The zpool vat stripes data across both providers. This creates a pool that contains two RAID-Z devices.

```
# zpool status vat
...
config:

NAME         STATE    READ   WRITE   CKSUM
vat          ONLINE   0      0       0
 raidz1-0    ONLINE   0      0       0
  gpt/zfs0   ONLINE   0      0       0
  gpt/zfs1   ONLINE   0      0       0
  gpt/zfs2   ONLINE   0      0       0
 raidz1-1    ONLINE   0      0       0
  gpt/zfs3   ONLINE   0      0       0
  gpt/zfs4   ONLINE   0      0       0
  gpt/zfs5   ONLINE   0      0       0
```

Each VDEV has its own redundancy.

While mirrors are faster than RAIDZ, you might find that the added speed of having multiple VDEVs makes this RAIDZ-based pool sufficiently fast for your workload and offers you significantly more space. The only way to tell is by creating the pool and testing your workload.

Remember, a pool splits all write requests between VDEVs in the pool. A single small file might only go to one VDEV, but in aggregate, writes are split between VDEVs. Using multiple VDEVs increases IOPS and throughput bandwidth.

Using Log Devices

As Chapter 2 discusses, ZFS can improve performance using dedicated write cache devices and/or dedicated read cache devices. These dedicated devices are normally very fast, high-endurance SSDs. The zpool(8) command calls the write cache a *log* and the read cache a *cache*.

Use the *log* and *cache* keywords to specify these devices when creating your pool. Here we create a striped pool, named scratch, with both a read and write cache.

```
# zpool create scratch gpt/zfs0 log gpt/zlog0 \
  cache gpt/zcache1
```

The log devices show up in the pool's status.

```
# zpool status scratch
...
config:

NAME            STATE    READ   WRITE   CKSUM
scratch         ONLINE      0       0       0
 gpt/zfs0       ONLINE      0       0       0
logs
 gpt/zlog0      ONLINE      0       0       0
cache
 gpt/zcache1    ONLINE      0       0       0
```

On systems that need high availability, you can mirror these write caches. Mirroring the read cache doesn't make much sense—if you lose the read cache, ZFS falls back to reading from the actual pool. Losing the ZIL write log can cause data loss, however, so mirroring it makes sense. Here we create a stripe of two mirrors using devices *gpt/zfs0* through *gpt/zfs3*, with mirrored log devices *gpt/zlog0* and *gpt/zlog1*.

```
# zpool create db mirror gpt/zfs0 gpt/zfs1 mirror \
  gpt/zfs2 gpt/zfs3 log mirror gpt/zlog0 gpt/zlog1
```

You can add intent log and read cache devices to an existing pool, or remove them. If you're not sure you need the performance boost of these devices, try running the pool without them. Make sure that your hardware has space to add SSD storage devices later, however!

Mismatched VDEVs

Using different VDEV types within a pool is not advisable, and zpool(8) attempts to prevent you from creating such a disaster.

```
# zpool create daftie raidz gpt/zfs0 gpt/zfs1 gpt/zfs2 \
  mirror gpt/zfs3 gpt/zfs4 gpt/zfs5
invalid vdev specification
use '-f' to override the following errors:
mismatched replication level: both raidz and mirror
vdevs are present
```

The `zpool(8)` command points out the mistake, and then tells you how to insist. We normally take these kinds of errors as a way of saying the sysadmin needs more caffeine, but maybe you really intended it. Running `zpool create -f` with the specified VDEV types and storage providers tells ZFS that yes, you fully intended to create a malformed pool. Hey, it's your system; you're in charge.

If ZFS doesn't want you to do something, you probably shouldn't. When you use `-f`, you're creating something that ZFS isn't designed to handle. You can easily create a pool that won't work well and *cannot* be repaired.

Reusing Providers

We sometimes create and destroy pools more than once to get them right. We might pull disks from one machine and mount them in another. Sometimes we encounter a disk that we've used before.

```
# zpool create db gpt/zfs1 gpt/zfs2 gpt/zfs3 gpt/zfs4
invalid vdev specification
use '-f' to override the following errors:
/dev/gpt/zfs3 is part of exported pool 'db'
```

We used this disk in another pool, which we later exported (see Chapter 5). The problem disk was used in that pool, and the ZFS label remained on the disk. While we erased and recreated the partition table, the new partition table happens to be precisely identical to the previous one. ZFS easily finds the old metadata in this case.

If you're absolutely sure this provider doesn't have anything important on it, follow the instructions and force creation of the new pool with -f.

```
# zpool create -f db gpt/zfs1 gpt/zfs2 gpt/zfs3 gpt/zfs4
```

The ZFS programs can be very picky about where your command-line flags go, so be sure the -f immediately follows create.

Pool Integrity

One common complaint about ZFS is that it has no filesystem checker, such as fsck(8). An offline file checker wouldn't improve ZFS because the online pool integrity checker verifies everything that fsck(8) checks for and more. The online checker is also much more effective than a traditional filesystem would ever let fsck(8) be. Let's talk about how ZFS ensures file integrity, and then how pool scrubbing helps maintain integrity.

ZFS Integrity

Storage devices screw up. When you have trillions of sectors on any sort of disk, the odds of a stray cosmic ray striking one hard enough to make it stagger around drunkenly go way up—as well as the odds of a write error, or a power failure, or a short in a faulty cable, or any number of other problems. No filesystem can prevent errors in the underlying hardware.

ZFS uses *hashes* almost everywhere. A hash is a mathematical algorithm that takes a chunk of data and computes a fixed-length string from it. The interesting thing about a hash is that minor changes in the original data dramatically change the hash of the data. Each block of storage includes the hash of its parent block, while each parent block includes the hash of all its children.

While ZFS cannot prevent storage provider errors, it uses these hashes to detect them. Whenever the system accesses data, it verifies the checksums. ZFS uses the pool's redundancy to repair any errors before giving the corrected file to the operating system. This is called *self-healing*.

If the underlying VDEVs have redundancy, ZFS either reconstructs the damaged block from RAID-Z or grabs the intact copy from the mirror. If both sides of a mirror have errors, ZFS can recover the files so long as the same data is not bad on both disks. If the VDEV has no redundancy, but a dataset has extra copies of the data (see Chapter 4), ZFS uses those extra copies instead.

If the underlying VDEV has no redundancy, and the dataset does not keep extra copies, the pool notes that the file is damaged and returns an error, instead of returning incorrect data. You can restore that file from backup, or throw it away.

While ZFS performs file integrity checks, it also verifies the connections between storage blocks. This is the task performed by `fsck(8)` in traditional filesystems. It's a small part of data verification, and ZFS performs this task continually as part of its normal operation. ZFS has an additional advantage over `fsck(8)` in that it checks only blocks that actually exist, rather than used and unused inodes. If you want to perform a full integrity check on all data in a pool, scrub it.

The nice thing about hash-based integrity checking is that it catches all sorts of errors, even unexpected ones. Remember, happy filesystems are all alike; every unhappy filesystem is unhappy in its own way.

Scrubbing ZFS

A *scrub* of a ZFS pool verifies the cryptographic hash of every data block in the pool. If the scrub detects an error, it repairs the error if sufficient resiliency exists. Scrubs happen while the pool is online and in use.

If your pool has identified any data errors, they'll show up in the zpool's status. If you've run a scrub before, you'll also see that information in the scan line.

```
...
scan: scrub repaired 0 in 15h57m with 0 errors on Sun
Feb  8 15:57:55 2015
...
errors: No known data errors
...
```

This pool has encountered no errors in the data it has accessed. If it had found errors, it would have self-healed them. The pool hasn't checked all the data for errors, however—it has checked only the data it's been asked for. To methodically search the entire pool for errors, use a *scrub*. Run `zpool scrub` and the pool name.

```
# zpool scrub zroot
```

Scrubs run in the background. You can see how they're doing by running `zpool status`.

```
# zpool status
...
scan: scrub in progress since Tue Feb 24 11:52:23 2015
  12.8G scanned out of 17.3G at 23.0M/s, 0h3m to go
  0 repaired, 74.08% done
...
```

A ZFS pool scrubbing its storage runs more slowly than usual. If your system is already pushing its performance limits, scrub pools only during off-peak hours. If you must cancel an ongoing scrub, run `zpool scrub -s`.

```
# zpool scrub -s zroot
```

Be sure to go back and have the system complete its scrub as soon as possible.

Scrub Frequency

ZFS' built-in integrity testing and resiliency mean that most errors are fixable, provided that they're found early enough for the resiliency to kick in. This means that your hardware's quality dictates how often you should scrub a host's pools. If you have reliable hardware, such as so-called "server grade" gear, scrubbing quarterly should suffice. If you're abusing cheap hardware, you should scrub every month or so.

FreeBSD can perform regular scrubs for you, as discussed in "ZFS Maintenance Automation" later this chapter.

Pool Properties

ZFS uses properties to express a pool's characteristics. While zpool properties look and work much like a dataset's properties, and many properties seem to overlap between the two, dataset properties have no relationship to pool properties. Pool properties include facts such as the pool's health, size, capacity, and per-pool features.

A pool's properties affect the entire pool. If you want to set a property for only part of a pool, check for a per-dataset property that fits your needs.

Viewing Pool Properties

To view all the properties of all the pools on your system, run `zpool get all`. You can add a pool name to the end if you want only the properties on a specific pool. Here we look at the properties for the pool `zroot`.

```
# zpool get all zroot
NAME    PROPERTY    VALUE    SOURCE
zroot   size        920G     -
zroot   capacity    1%       -
zroot   altroot     -        default
zroot   health      ONLINE   -
...
```

The first two columns give the pool name and the name of the property.

The third column lists the value of the property. This can be something like *enabled* or *disabled,* *on* or *off, active* or *inactive,* or it can be a value. This pool's `size` property is 920G—this pool has 920 GB of space.

The SOURCE column shows where this property is set. This can be a single dash, or the words *default* or *local.* A dash means that this property isn't set per se, but rather somehow read from the pool. You don't set the value for the pool's size or how much of that space is used. FreeBSD calculates those values from the pool. A SOURCE of default indicates that this property is set to its default value, while local means that this property has been specifically set on this pool.

To get a single property, run `zpool get` with the property name.

```
# zpool get size
NAME     PROPERTY   VALUE   SOURCE
db       size       2.72T   -
zroot    size       920G    -
```

Narrow this down by giving the pool name at the end.

Changing Pool Properties

We'll set properties throughout this book to change pool behavior. Change a pool's properties using the `zpool set` command. Here we set a pool's `comment` property.

```
# zpool set comment="Main OS files" zroot
```

This comment now appears within the property list.

```
# zpool get comment
NAME     PROPERTY   VALUE           SOURCE
db       comment    -               default
zroot    comment    Main OS files   local
```

Note the SOURCE column here. By default, pools have no comment. Now that I've set a comment, though, the source changes to local. Once a property's source changes from default to local, it remains local forever. Even setting the property to the default value won't change the source.

```
# zpool set comment="-" zroot
# zpool get comment
NAME    PROPERTY   VALUE   SOURCE
db      comment    -       default
zroot   comment    -       local
```

We locally set the comment to the default value, so the value's source remains local.

You can set a pool's properties at creation time with -o. You can set properties for the root dataset on that pool with -o.

```
# zpool create -o altroot=/mnt -O canmount=off \
  -m none zroot /dev/gpt/disk0
```

The pool has its **altroot** property set to /mnt, and the root dataset on this pool has the **canmount** property set to *off*. If a property changes how data is written, only data written after changing the property is affected. ZFS won't rewrite existing data to comply with a property change.

Pool History

Every zpool retains a copy of all changes that have ever been made to the pool, all the way back to the pool's creation. This history doesn't include routine events like system power-on and power-off, but it does include setting properties, pool upgrades, and dataset creation.

To access the history, run zpool history and give the pool name.

```
# zpool history zroot
History for 'zroot':
2014-01-07.04:12:05 zpool create -o altroot=/mnt -O can-
mount=off -m none zroot mirror /dev/gpt/disk0.nop /dev/
gpt/disk1.nop
2014-01-07.04:12:50 zfs set checksum=fletcher4 zroot
2014-01-07.04:13:00 zfs set atime=off zroot
...
```

Experienced FreeBSD hands probably recognize this from any number of ZFS tutorials in the FreeBSD documentation and forums.

The history ends with:

```
...
2015-03-12.14:36:35 zpool set comment=Main OS files
zroot
2015-03-12.14:43:45 zpool set comment=- zroot
```

We changed the **comment** property, so it's in the history. Forever.

Sadly, the pool history doesn't track who made each change, but having a permanent record of changes helps with problem analysis.

Zpool Maintenance Automation

FreeBSD checks each system's filesystems as part of the daily maintenance job run by periodic(8). You can add ZFS pool information to this check, so that you'll get information on pool health. The daily_status_zfs_enable *periodic.conf* option enables pool checks.

```
daily_status_zfs_enable="YES"
```

The daily periodic(8) output now includes the output of zpool status -x, which is normally the single line of "all pools are healthy."

If you want more detailed information on your pools, the daily report can also include zpool list output. Set daily_status_zfs_zpool_list to YES to get the list. If you want to trim that output, showing only the status of specific pools, list the desired pools in the daily_status_zpool *periodic.conf* variable.

You can also have FreeBSD perform your pool scrubs. With the scrubbing options set, FreeBSD performs a daily check to see if the pool needs scrubbing, but only scrubs at configured intervals. To automatically scrub every pool every 35 days, set daily_scrub_zfs_enable to YES in *periodic.conf*.

```
daily_scrub_zfs_enable="YES"
```

FreeBSD defaults to scrubbing all pools. You can't explicitly exclude specific pools from the daily scrub check. You can, however, explicitly list the pools you want checked in daily_scrub_zfs_pools. Any pool not listed isn't scrubbed.

```
daily_scrub_zfs_pools="zroot prod test"
```

To change the number of days between scrubs, set daily_scrub_zfs_default_threshold to the desired number of days.

```
daily_scrub_zfs_default_threshold="10"
```

If you want to scrub a specific pool on a different schedule, set daily_scrub_zfs_${poolname}_threshold to the desired number of days. Here we scrub the pool *prod* every 7 days.

```
daily_scrub_zfs_prod_threshold="7"
```

Any pool without its own personal threshold uses the default threshold.

Removing Pools

To get rid of a pool, use the `zpool destroy` command and the pool name.

```
# zpool destroy test
```

Destruction marks the pool's underlying providers as being part of a destroyed pool, so that they can be reused for other pools. It does not erase the disks, and anyone who has read Chapter 5 can restore the pool and access the data.

If you must securely erase or overwrite the data on the providers, you'll need a disk overwriting or shredding program.

Zpool Feature Flags

ZFS and pools originally came with a version number, indicating the features supported by the pool. A system could look at an unfamiliar storage provider and say, "Oh, this pool is ZFS version 20, so it doesn't support deduplication or native encryption." You could upgrade the pool to the newest version supported by your release—or not.

Then Oracle closed the ZFS source, leaving various people to pick up the last open-source ZFS release and maintain it on their own. The final open-source Oracle ZFS version was 28. As various groups implemented their own pool features, version numbers from different groups threatened to become mutually incompatible. Different ZFS teams could implement whatever new features they chose, meaning that, say, FooZFS version 30 would be incompatibly with BarZFS version 30. A major goal of ZFS is interoperability.

The OpenZFS team decided that the best way forward was to break away from tracking features with version numbers. They cranked the OpenZFS version up to 5000, leaving Oracle plenty of room to add new versions. To accommodate all the different OpenZFS developers on all the different platforms, the developers chose to effectively replace the version numbers with *feature flags*.

Every platform that runs OpenZFS, including FreeBSD, should include a `zpool-features(7)` manual page that lists the pool features this particular install supports. Newer versions of FreeBSD will probably support new pool features.

Using a feature normally changes the on-disk format in some way. Adding snapshot support, for example, means adding new fields and metadata to say "this is a snapshot." A system that doesn't support that feature will look at this pool and go "oh crud, I don't recognize that data structure. I ain't touching this!" If you routinely swap disks between systems, you'll want to carefully check feature flags supported on the various hosts before upgrading or enabling new feature flags.

Viewing Feature Flags

To view the feature flags supported by a pool, and their settings, look for pool properties that include the word "feature."

```
# zpool get all zroot | grep feature
zroot   feature@async_destroy   enabled   local
zroot   feature@empty_bpobj     active    local
zroot   feature@lz4_compress    active    local
...
```

Pool features that are *enabled* are available for use, but not actually used yet. Your system might support a new type of compression, but has not actually written any data to the pool using the new algorithm. This pool could be imported on a system that doesn't support the feature, because the on-disk format has not changed to accommodate the feature. The new host won't see anything that makes it freak out.

Disabled pool features are available in the operating system but not enabled. Nothing in the pool says that these features are available—the presence of disabled features means they're available in the operating system. This pool is definitely usable on hosts that don't support this feature.

If the feature is *active*, the on-disk format has changed because the feature is in use. Most commonly, this pool cannot be imported onto a system that doesn't support this feature. If the feature is active, but all datasets using the feature are destroyed, the pool reverts the feature setting to *enabled*.

A few features are "read-only compatible." If the feature is in active use, the pool could be partially imported onto a system that doesn't support the feature. The new host might not see some datasets on the pool, and it can't write any data to the pool, but it might be able to extract some data from the datasets.

Creating a pool enables all features supported by that operating system's ZFS implementation. You could use the -d flag with `zpool create` to disable all features in a new pool and then enable features more selectively.

Now that you understand how pools work, let's put some actual data on them.

Chapter 4: ZFS Datasets

With ordinary filesystems you create partitions to separate different types of data, apply different optimizations to them, and limit how much of your space the partition can consume. Each partition receives a specific amount of space from the disk. We've all been there. We make our best guesses at how much disk space each partition on this system will need next month, next year, and five years from now. Fast forward to the future, and the amount of space you decided to give each partition is more than likely wrong. A partition without enough space for all its data sends you adding disks or moving data, complicating system management. When a partition has too much space, you kick yourself and use it as a dumping ground for stuff you'd rather have elsewhere. More than one of Lucas' UFS2 systems has `/usr/ports` as a symlink to somewhere in `/home`. Jude usually ends up with some part of `/var` living in `/usr/local/var`.

ZFS solves this problem by *pooling* free space, giving your partitions flexibility impossible with more common filesystems. Each ZFS dataset you create consumes only the space required to store the files within it. Each dataset has access to all of the free space in the pool, eliminating your worries about the size of your partitions. You can limit the size of a dataset with a quota or guarantee it a minimum amount of space with a reservation, as discussed in Chapter 6.

Regular filesystems use the separate partitions to establish different policies and optimizations for the different types of data. /var contains often-changing files like logs and databases. The root filesystem needs consistency and safety over performance. Over in /home, anything goes. Once you establish a policy for a traditional filesystem, though, it's really hard to change. The tunefs(8) utility for UFS requires the filesystem be unmounted to make changes. Some characteristics, such as the number of inodes, just cannot be changed after the filesystem has been created.

The core problem of traditional filesystems distills to inflexibility. ZFS datasets are almost infinitely flexible.

Datasets

A dataset is a named chunk of data. This data might resemble a traditional filesystem, with files, directories, and permissions and all that fun stuff. It could be a raw block device, or a copy of other data, or anything you can cram onto a disk.

ZFS uses datasets much like a traditional filesystem might use partitions. Need a policy for /usr and a separate policy for /home? Make each a dataset. Need a block device for an iSCSI target? That's a dataset. Want a copy of a dataset? That's another dataset.

Datasets have a hierarchical relationship. A single storage pool is the parent of each top-level dataset. Each dataset can have child datasets. Datasets inherit many characteristics from their parent, as we'll see throughout this chapter.

You'll perform all dataset operations with the zfs(8) command. This command has all sorts of sub-commands.

Dataset Types

ZFS currently has five types of datasets: filesystems, volumes, snapshots, clones, and bookmarks.

A *filesystem* dataset resembles a traditional filesystem. It stores files and directories. A ZFS filesystem has a mount point and supports traditional filesystem characteristics like read-only, restricting setuid binaries, and more. Filesystem datasets also hold other information, including permissions, timestamps for file creation and modification, NFSv4 Access Control Flags, chflags(2), and the like.

A *ZFS volume*, or *zvol*, is a block device. In an ordinary filesystem, you might create a file-backed filesystem for iSCSI or a special-purpose UFS partition. On ZFS, these block devices bypass all the overhead of files and directories and reside directly on the underlying pool. Zvols get a device node, skipping the FreeBSD memory devices used to mount disk images.

A *snapshot* is a read-only copy of a dataset from a specific point in time. Snapshots let you retain previous versions of your filesystem and the files therein for later use. Snapshots use an amount of space based on the difference between the current filesystem and what's in the snapshot.

A *clone* is a new dataset based on a snapshot of an existing dataset, allowing you to fork a filesystem. You get an extra copy of everything in the dataset. You might clone the dataset containing your production web site, giving you a copy of the site that you can hack on without touching the production site. A clone only consumes space to store the differences from the original snapshot it was created from. Chapter 7 covers snapshots, clones, and bookmarks.

Why Do I Want Datasets?

You obviously need datasets. Putting files on the disk requires a filesystem dataset. And you probably want a dataset for each traditional Unix partition, like /usr and /var. But with ZFS, you want a lot of datasets. Lots and lots and *lots* of datasets. This would be cruel madness with a traditional filesystem, with its hard-coded limits on the number of partitions and the inflexibility of those partitions. But using many datasets increases the control you have over your data.

Each ZFS dataset has a series of properties that control its operation, allowing the administrator to control how the dataset performs and how carefully it protects its data. You can tune each dataset exactly as you can with a traditional filesystem. Dataset properties work much like pool properties.

The sysadmin can delegate control over individual datasets to another user, allow the user to manage it without root privileges. If your organization has a whole bunch of project teams, you can give each project manager their own chunk of space and say, "Here, arrange it however you want." Anything that reduces our workload is a good thing.

Many ZFS features, such as replication and snapshots, operate on a per-dataset basis. Separating your data into logical groups makes it easier to use these ZFS features to support your organization.

Take the example of a web server with dozens of sites, each maintained by different teams. Some teams are responsible for multiple sites, while others have only one. Some people belong to multiple teams. If you follow the traditional filesystem model, you might create a /webserver dataset, put everything in it, and control access with group permissions and sudo(8). You've lived like this for decades, and it works, so why change?

But create a dataset for each team, and give each site its own dataset within that parent dataset, and possibilities multiply.

A team needs a copy of a web site for testing? Clone it. With traditional filesystems, you'd have to copy the whole site directory, doubling the amount of disk needed for the site and taking much, much longer. A clone uses only the amount of space for the differences between the sites and appears instantaneously.

The team is about to deploy a new version of a site, but wants a backup of the old site? Create a snapshot. This new site probably uses a whole bunch of the same files as the old one, so you'll reduce disk space usage. Plus, when the deployment goes horribly wrong, you can restore the old version by rolling back to the snapshot.

A particular web site needs filesystem-level performance tweaks, or compression, or some locally created property? Set it for that site.

You might create a dataset for each team, and then let the teams create their own child datasets for their own sites. You can organize your datasets to fit your people, rather than organizing your people to fit your technology.

When you must change a filesystem setting (property) on all of the sites, make the change to the parent dataset and let the children inherit it.

The same benefits apply to user home directories.

You can also move datasets between machines. Your web sites overflow the web server? Send half the datasets, along with their custom settings and all their clones and snapshots, to the new server.

There is one disadvantage to using many filesystem datasets. When you move a file within a filesystem, the file is renamed. Moving files between separate filesystems requires copying the file to a new location and deleting it from the old, rather than just renaming it. Inter-dataset file copies take more time and require more free space. But that's trivial against all the benefits ZFS gives you with multiple datasets. This problem exists on other filesystems as well, but hosts using most other filesystems have only a few partitions, making it less obvious.

Viewing Datasets

The `zfs list` command shows all of the datasets, and some basic information about them.

```
# zfs list
NAME                       USED   AVAIL  REFER  MOUNTPOINT
mypool                     420M   17.9G    96K  none
mypool/ROOT                418M   17.9G    96K  none
mypool/ROOT/default 418M   17.9G   418M  /
...
```

The first field shows the dataset's name.

Under USED and REFER you find information about how much disk space the dataset uses. One downside to ZFS' incredible flexibility and efficiency is that its interpretation of disk space usage seems somewhat surreal if you don't understand it. Chapter 6 discusses disk space and strategies to use it.

The AVAIL column shows how much space remains free in the pool or dataset.

Finally MOUNTPOINT shows where the dataset should be mounted. That doesn't mean that the dataset is mounted, merely that if it were to be mounted, this is where it would go. (Use `zfs mount` to see all mounted ZFS filesystems.)

If you give a dataset as an argument, `zfs list` shows only that specific dataset.

```
# zfs list mypool/lamb
NAME          USED   AVAIL  REFER  MOUNTPOINT
mypool/lamb   192K   17.9G    96K  /lamb
```

Restrict the type of dataset shown with the -t flag and the type. You can show filesystems, volumes, or snapshots. Here we display snapshots, and only snapshots.

```
# zfs list -t snapshot
NAME                        USED  AVAIL  REFER  MOUNTPOINT
zroot/var/log/db@backup       0      -  10.0G  -
```

Now that you can see filesystems, let's make some.

Creating, Moving, and Destroying Datasets

Use the `zfs create` command to create any dataset. We'll look at snapshots, clones, and bookmarks in Chapter 7, but let's discuss filesystems and volumes now.

Creating Filesystems

Filesystems are the most common type of dataset on most systems. Everyone needs a place to store and organize files. Create a filesystem dataset by specifying the pool and the filesystem name.

```
# zfs create mypool/lamb
```

This creates a new dataset, *lamb*, on the ZFS pool called *mypool*. If the pool has a default mount point, the new dataset is mounted by default (see "Mounting ZFS Filesystems" later this chapter).

```
# mount | grep lamb
mypool/lamb on /lamb (zfs, local, noatime, nfsv4acls)
```

The mount settings in parentheses are usually ZFS properties, inherited from the parent dataset. To create a child filesystem, give the full path to the parent filesystem.

```
# zfs create mypool/lamb/baby
```

The dataset inherits many of its characteristics, including its mount point, from the parent, as we'll see in "Parent/Child Relationships" later in this chapter.

Creating Volumes

Use the -v flag and a volume size to tell `zfs create` that you want to create a volume. Give the full path to the volume dataset.

```
# zfs create -V 4G mypool/avolume
```

Zvols show up in a dataset list like any other dataset. You can tell `zfs list` to show only zvols by adding the `-t volume` option.

```
# zfs list mypool/avolume
NAME              USED  AVAIL  REFER  MOUNTPOINT
mypool/avolume    4.13G  17.9G   64K   -
```

Zvols automatically reserve an amount of space equal to the size of the volume plus the ZFS metadata. This 4 GB zvol uses 4.13 GB of space.

As block devices, zvols do not have a mount point. They do get a device node under */dev/zvol*, so you can access them as you would any other block device.

```
# ls -al /dev/zvol/mypool/avolume
crw-r----- 1 root operator  0x4d Mar 27 20:22 /dev/zvol/mypool/avolume
```

You can run `newfs(8)` on this device node, copy a disk image to it, and generally use it like any other block device.

Renaming Datasets

You can rename a dataset with, oddly enough, the `zfs rename` command. Give the dataset's current name as the first argument and the new location as the second.

```
# zfs rename db/production db/old
# zfs rename db/testing db/production
```

Use the -f flag to forcibly rename the dataset. You cannot unmount a filesystem with processes running in it, but the -f flag gleefully forces the unmount. Any process using the dataset loses access to whatever it was using, and reacts however it will.[9]

9   Probably badly.

Moving Datasets

You can move a dataset from part of the ZFS tree to another, making the dataset a child of its new parent. This may cause many of the dataset's properties to change, since children inherit properties from their parent. Any properties set specifically on the dataset will not change.

Here we move a database out from under the `zroot/var/db` dataset, to a new parent where you have set some properties to improve fault tolerance.

```
# zfs rename zroot/var/db/mysql zroot/important/mysql
```

Note that since mount points are inherited, this will likely change the dataset's mount point. Adding the -u flag to the `rename` command will cause ZFS not to immediately change the mount point, giving you time to reset the property to the intended value. Remember that if the machine is restarted, or the dataset is manually remounted, it will use its new mount point.

You can rename a snapshot, but you cannot move snapshots out of their parent dataset. Snapshots are covered in detail in Chapter 7.

Destroying Datasets

Sick of that dataset? Drag it out behind the barn and put it out of your misery with `zfs destroy`.

```
# zfs destroy db/old
```

If you add the -r flag, you recursively destroy all children (datasets, snapshots, etc.) of the dataset. To destroy any cloned datasets while you're at it, use -R. Be very careful recursively destroying datasets, as you can frequently be surprised by what, exactly, is a child of a dataset.

You might use the -v and -n flags to see exactly what will happen when you destroy a dataset. The -v flag prints verbose information about what gets destroyed, while -n tells `zfs(8)` to perform a dry run. Between the two, they show what this command would actually destroy before you pull the trigger.

ZFS Properties

ZFS datasets have a number of settings, called *properties*, that control how the dataset works. While you can set a few of these only when you create the dataset, most of them are tunable while the dataset is live. ZFS also offers a number of read-only properties that provide information such as the amount of space consumed by the dataset, the compression or deduplication ratios, and the creation time of the dataset.

Each dataset inherits its properties from its parent, unless the property is specifically set on that dataset.

Viewing Properties

The `zfs(8)` tool can retrieve a specific property, or all properties for a dataset. Use the `zfs get` command, the desired property, and if desired, a dataset name.

```
# zfs get compression mypool/lamb
NAME            PROPERTY      VALUE   SOURCE
mypool/lamb   compression   lz4      inherited from mypool
```

Under NAME we see the dataset you asked about, and PROPERTY shows the property you requested. The VALUE is what the property is set to.

The SOURCE is a little more complicated. A source of *default* means that this property is set to ZFS' default. A *local* source means that someone deliberately set this property on this dataset. A *temporary* property was set when the dataset was mounted, and this property reverts to its usual value when the dataset is unmounted. An *inherited* property comes from a parent dataset, as discussed in "Parent/Child Relationships" later in this chapter.

Some properties have no source because the source is either irrelevant or inherently obvious. The creation property, which records the date and time the dataset was created, has no source. The value came from the system clock.

If you don't specify a dataset name, `zfs get` shows the value of this property for all datasets. The special property keyword *all* retrieves all of a dataset's properties.

```
# zfs get all mypool/lamb
NAME            PROPERTY     VALUE                   SOURCE
mypool/lamb     type         filesystem              -
mypool/lamb     creation     Fri Mar 27 20:05 2015   -
mypool/lamb     used         192K                    -
...
```

If you use *all* and don't give a dataset name, you get all the properties for all datasets. This is a lot of information.

Show multiple properties by separating the property names with commas.

```
# zfs get quota,reservation zroot/home
NAME         PROPERTY      VALUE    SOURCE
zroot/home   quota         none     local
zroot/home   reservation   none     default
```

You can also view properties with `zfs list` and the `-o` modifier. This is most suited for when you want to view several properties from multiple datasets. Use the special property **name** to show the dataset's name.

```
# zfs list -o name,quota,reservation
NAME                QUOTA   RESERV
db                  none    none
zroot               none    none
zroot/ROOT          none    none
zroot/ROOT/default  none    none
...
zroot/var/log       100G    20G
...
```

You can also add a dataset name to see these properties in this format for that dataset.

Changing Properties

Change properties with the `zfs set` command. Give the property name, the new setting, and the dataset name. Here we change the **compression** property to *off*.

```
# zfs set compression=off mypool/lamb/baby
```

Confirm your change with `zfs get`.

```
# zfs get compression mypool/lamb/baby
NAME                 PROPERTY      VALUE   SOURCE
mypool/lamb/baby     compression   off     local
```

Most properties apply only to data written after the property is changed. The **compression** property tells ZFS to compress data before writing it to disk. We talk about compression in Chapter 6. Disabling compression doesn't uncompress any data written before the change was made. Similarly, enabling compression doesn't magically compress data already on the disk. To get the full benefit of enabling compression, you must rewrite every file. You're better off creating a new dataset, copying the data over with `zfs send`, and destroying the original dataset.

Read-Only Properties

ZFS uses read-only properties to offer basic information about the dataset. Disk space usage is expressed as properties. You can't change how much data you're using by changing the property that says "your disk is half-full." (Chapter 6 covers ZFS disk space usage.) The **creation** property records when this dataset was created. You can change many read-only properties by adding or removing data to the disk, but you can't write these properties directly.

Filesystem Properties

One key tool for managing the performance and behavior of traditional filesystems is mount options. You can mount traditional filesystems read-only, or use the `noexec` flag to disable running programs from them. ZFS uses properties to achieve the same effects. Here are the properties used to accomplish these familiar goals.

atime

A file's atime indicates when the file was last accessed. ZFS' **atime** property controls whether the dataset tracks access times. The default value, *on*, updates the file's atime metadata every time the file is accessed. Using **atime** means writing to the disk every time it's read.

Turning this property off avoids writing to the disk when you read a file, and can result in significant performance gains. It might confuse mailers and other similar utilities that depend on being able to determine when a file was last read.

Leaving **atime** on increases snapshot size. The first time a file is accessed, its atime is updated. The snapshot retains the original access time, while the live filesystem contains the newly updated accessed time. This is the default.

exec

The **exec** property determines if anyone can run binaries and commands on this filesystem. The default is *on*, which permits execution. Some environments don't permit users to execute programs from their personal or temporary directories. Set the **exec** property to *off* to disable execution of programs on the filesystem.

The **exec** property doesn't prohibit people from running interpreted scripts, however. If a user can run */bin/sh*, they can run */bin/sh / home/mydir/script.sh*. The shell is what's actually executing—it only takes instructions from the script.

readonly

If you don't want anything writing to this dataset, set the `readonly` property to *on*. The default, *off*, lets users modify the dataset within administrative permissions.

setuid

Many people consider setuid programs risky.[10] While some programs must be setuid, such as `passwd(1)` and `login(1)`, there's rarely a need to have setuid programs on filesystems like */home* and */tmp*. Many sysadmins disallow setuid programs except on specific filesystems.

ZFS' `setuid` property toggles setuid support. If set to *on*, the filesystem supports setuid. If set to *off*, the `setuid` flag is ignored.

User-Defined Properties

ZFS properties are great, and you can't get enough of them, right? Well, start adding your own. The ability to store your own metadata along with your datasets lets you develop whole new realms of automation. The fact that children automatically inherit these properties makes life even easier.

To make sure your custom properties remain yours, and don't conflict with other people's custom properties, create a namespace. Most people prefix their custom properties with an organizational identifier and a colon. For example, FreeBSD-specific properties have the format "org.freebsd:propertyname," such as `org.freebsd:swap`. If the illumos project creates its own property named *swap*, they'd call it `org.illumos:swap`. The two values won't collide.

---

10   Properly written setuid programs are not risky. That's why real setuid programs are risky.

For example, suppose Jude wants to control which datasets get backed up via a dataset property. He creates the namespace `com.allan-jude`.[11] Within that namespace, he creates the property `backup_ignore`.

```
# zfs set com.allanjude:backup_ignore=on mypool/lamb
```

Jude's backup script checks the value of this property. If it's set to *true*, the backup process skips this dataset.

Parent/Child Relationships

Datasets inherit properties from their parent datasets. When you set a property on a dataset, that property applies to that dataset and all of its children. For convenience, you can run `zfs(8)` commands on a dataset and all of its children by adding the `-r` flag. Here, we query the **compression** property on a dataset and all of its children.

```
# zfs get -r compression mypool/lamb
NAME                 PROPERTY      VALUE  SOURCE
mypool/lamb          compression   lz4    inherited from mypool
mypool/lamb/baby     compression   off    local
```

Look at the source values. The first dataset, *mypool/lamb*, inherited this property from the parent pool. In the second dataset, this property has a different value. The source is local, meaning that the property was set specifically on this dataset.

We can restore the original setting with the `zfs inherit` command.

```
# zfs inherit compression mypool/lamb/baby
# zfs get -r compression mypool/lamb
NAME                 PROPERTY      VALUE  SOURCE
mypool/lamb          compression   lz4    inherited from mypool
mypool/lamb/baby     compression   lz4    inherited from mypool
```

The child now inherits the **compression** properties from the parent, which inherits from the grandparent.

---

11   When you name ZFS properties after yourself, you are immortalized by your work. Whether this is good or bad depends on your work.

When you change a parent's properties, the new properties auto-matically propagate down to the child.

```
# zfs set compression=gzip-9 mypool/lamb
# zfs get -r compression mypool/lamb
NAME                   PROPERTY       VALUE  SOURCE
mypool/lamb            compression    gzip-9 local
mypool/lamb/baby       compression    gzip-9 inherited from mypool/lamb
```

I told the parent dataset to use *gzip-9* compression. That percolated down to the child.

Inheritance and Renaming

When you move or rename a dataset so that it has a new parent, the parent's properties automatically propagate down to the child. Locally set properties remain unchanged, but inherited ones switch to those from the new parent.

Here we create a new parent dataset and check its **compression** property.

```
# zfs create mypool/second
# zfs get compress mypool/second
NAME              PROPERTY       VALUE SOURCE
mypool/second     compression    lz4   inherited from mypool
```

Our *baby* dataset uses *gzip-9* compression. It's inherited this prop-erty from *mypool/lamb*. Now let's move *baby* to be a child of *second*, and see what happens to the **compression** property.

```
# zfs rename mypool/lamb/baby mypool/second/baby
# zfs get -r compression mypool/second
NAME                   PROPERTY       VALUE  SOURCE
mypool/second          compression    lz4    inherited from mypool
mypool/second/baby     compression    lz4    inherited from mypool
```

The child dataset now belongs to a different parent, and inherits its properties from the new parent. The child keeps any local properties.

Data on the baby dataset is a bit of a tangle, however. Data writ-ten before **compression** was turned on is uncompressed. Data written while the dataset used gzip-9 compression is compressed with gzip-9.

Any data written now will be compressed with lz4. ZFS sorts all this out for you automatically, but thinking about it does make one's head hurt.

Removing Properties

While you can set a property back to its default value, it's not obvious how to change the source back to *inherit* or *default*, or how to remove custom properties once they're set.

To remove a custom property, inherit it.

```
# zfs inherit com.allanjude:backup_ignore mypool/lamb
```

This works even if you set the property on the root dataset.

To reset a property to its default value on a dataset and all its children, or totally remove custom properties, use the zfs inherit command on the pool's root dataset.

```
# zfs inherit -r compression mypool
```

It's counterintuitive, but it knocks the custom setting off of the root dataset.

Mounting ZFS Filesystems

With traditional filesystems you listed each partition, its type, and where it should be mounted in /etc/fstab. You even listed temporary mounts such as floppies and CD-ROM drives, just for convenience. ZFS allows you to create such a large number of filesystems that this quickly grows impractical.

Each ZFS filesystem has a `mountpoint` property that defines where it should be mounted. The default `mountpoint` is built from the pool's `mountpoint`. If a pool doesn't have a mount point, you must assign a mount point to any datasets you want to mount.

```
# zfs get mountpoint zroot/usr/home
NAME              PROPERTY      VALUE       SOURCE
zroot/usr/home    mountpoint    /usr/home   inherited from zroot/usr
```

The filesystem normally get mounted at */usr/home*. You could override this when manually mounting the filesystem.

The *zroot* pool used for a default FreeBSD install doesn't have a mount point set. If you create new datasets directly under *zroot*, they won't have a mount point. Datasets created on zroot under, say, */usr*, inherit a mount point from their parent dataset.

Any pool other than the pool with the root filesystem normally has a mount point named after the pool. If you create a pool named *db*, it gets mounted at */db*. All children inherit their mount point from that pool unless you change them.

When you change the **mountpoint** property for a filesystem, the filesystem and any children that inherit the mount point are unmounted. If the new value is *legacy*, then they remain unmounted. Otherwise, they are automatically remounted in the new location if the property was previously *legacy* or *none*, or if they were mounted before the property was changed. In addition, any shared filesystems are unshared and shared in the new location.

Just like ordinary filesystems, ZFS filesystems aren't necessarily mounted. The **canmount** property controls a filesystem's mount behavior. If **canmount** is set to *yes*, running zfs mount -a mounts the filesystem, just like mount -a. When you enable ZFS in */etc/rc.conf*, FreeBSD runs zfs mount -a at startup.

When the **canmount** property is set to *noauto*, a dataset can only be mounted and unmounted explicitly. The dataset is not mounted automatically when the dataset is created or imported, nor is it mounted by the zfs mount -a command or unmounted by zfs unmount -a.

Things can get interesting when you set **canmount** to *off*. You might have two non-mountable datasets with the same mount point. A dataset can exist solely for the purpose of being the parent to future datasets, but not actually store files, as we'll see below.

Child datasets do not inherit the **canmount** property.

Changing the **canmount** property does not automatically unmount or mount the filesystem. If you disable mounting on a mounted filesystem, you'll need to manually unmount the filesystem or reboot.

Datasets without Mount Points

ZFS datasets are hierarchical. You might need to create a dataset that will never contain any files only so it can be the common parent of a number of other datasets. Consider a default install of FreeBSD 10.1 or newer.

```
# zfs mount
zroot/ROOT/default    /
zroot/tmp             /tmp
zroot/usr/home        /usr/home
zroot/usr/ports       /usr/ports
zroot/usr/src         /usr/src
...
```

We have all sorts of datasets under /usr, but there's no /usr dataset mounted. What's going on?

A zfs list shows that a dataset exists, and it has a mount point of /usr. But let's check the **mountpoint** and **canmount** properties of *zroot/usr* and all its children.

```
# zfs list -o name,canmount,mountpoint -r zroot/usr
NAME               CANMOUNT  MOUNTPOINT
zroot/usr               off  /usr
zroot/usr/home           on  /usr/home
zroot/usr/ports          on  /usr/ports
zroot/usr/src            on  /usr/src
```

With `canmount` set to *off*, the *zroot/usr* dataset is never mounted. Any files written in */usr*, such as the commands in */usr/bin* and the packages in */usr/local*, go into the root filesystem. Lower-level mount points such as */usr/src* have their own datasets, which are mounted.

The dataset exists only to be a parent to the child datasets. You'll see something similar with the */var* partitions.

Multiple Datasets with the Same Mount Point

Setting `canmount` to *off* allows datasets to be used solely as a mechanism to inherit properties. One reason to set `canmount` to *off* is to have two datasets with the same mount point, so that the children of both datasets appear in the same directory, but might have different inherited characteristics.

FreeBSD's installer does not have a `mountpoint` on the default pool, *zroot*. When you create a new dataset, you must assign a mount point to it.

If you don't want to assign a mount point to every dataset you create right under the pool, you might assign a `mountpoint` of / to the *zroot* pool and leave `canmount` set to *off*. This way, when you create a new dataset, it has a `mountpoint` to inherit. This is a very simple example of using multiple datasets with the same mount point.

Imagine you want an */opt* directory with two sets of subdirectories. Some of these directories contain programs, and should never be written to after installation. Other directories contain data. You must lock down the ability to run programs at the filesystem level.

```
# zfs create db/programs
# zfs create db/data
```

Now give both of these datasets the `mountpoint` of */opt* and tell them that they cannot be mounted.

```
# zfs set canmount=off db/programs
# zfs set mountpoint=/opt db/programs
```

Install your programs to the dataset, and then make it read-only.

```
# zfs set readonly=on db/programs
```

You can't run programs from the *db/data* dataset, so turn off **exec** and **setuid**. We need to write data to these directories, however.

```
# zfs set canmount=off db/data
# zfs set mountpoint=/opt db/data
# zfs set setuid=off db/data
# zfs set exec=off db/data
```

Now create some child datasets. The children of the *db/programs* dataset inherit that dataset's properties, while the children of the *db/data* dataset inherit the other set of properties.

```
# zfs create db/programs/bin
# zfs create db/programs/sbin
# zfs create db/data/test
# zfs create db/data/production
```

We now have four datasets mounted inside */opt*, two for binaries and two for data. As far as users know, these are normal directories. No matter what the file permissions say, though, nobody can write to two of these directories. Regardless of what trickery people pull, the system won't recognize executables and setuid files in the other two. When you need another dataset for data or programs, create it as a child of the dataset with the desired settings. Changes to the parent datasets propagate immediately to all the children.

Pools without Mount Points

While a pool is normally mounted at a directory named after the pool, that isn't necessarily so.

```
# zfs set mountpoint=none mypool
```

This pool no longer gets mounted. Neither does any dataset on the pool unless you specify a mount point. This is how the FreeBSD installer creates the pool for the OS.

```
# zfs set mountpoint=/someplace mypool/lamb
```

The directory will be created if necessary and the filesystem mounted.

Manually Mounting and Unmounting Filesystems

To manually mount a filesystem, use `zfs mount` and the dataset name. This is most commonly used for filesystems with **canmount** set to *noauto*.

```
# zfs mount mypool/usr/src
```

To unmount a filesystem and all of its children, use `zfs unmount`.

```
# zfs unmount mypool/second
```

If you want to temporarily mount a dataset at a different location, use the `-o` flag to specify a new mount point. This mount point only lasts until you unmount the dataset.

```
# zfs mount -o mountpoint=/mnt mypool/lamb
```

You can only mount a dataset if it has a **mountpoint** defined. Defining a temporary mount point when the dataset has no mount point gives you an error.

ZFS and /etc/fstab

You can choose to manage some or all of your ZFS filesystem mount points with */etc/fstab* if you prefer. Set the dataset's **mountpoint** property to *legacy*. This unmounts the filesystem.

```
# zfs set mountpoint=legacy mypool/second
```

Now you can mount this dataset with the mount(8) command:

```
# mount -t zfs mypool/second /tmp/second
```

You can also add ZFS datasets to the system's /etc/fstab. Use the full dataset name as the device node. Set the type to *zfs*. You can use the standard filesystem options of noatime, noexec, readonly or ro, and nosuid. (You could also explicitly give the default behaviors of atime, exec, rw, and suid, but these are ZFS' defaults.) The mount order is normal, but the fsck field is ignored. Here's an /etc/fstab entry that mounts the dataset *scratch/junk* nosuid at /tmp.

```
scratch/junk  /tmp  nosuid  2  0
```

We recommend using ZFS properties to manage your mounts, however. Properties can do almost everything /etc/fstab does, and more.

Tweaking ZFS Volumes

Zvols are pretty straightforward—here's a chunk of space as a block device; use it. You can adjust how a volume uses space and what kind of device node it offers.

Space Reservations

The **volsize** property of a zvol specifies the volume's logical size. By default, creating a volume reserves an amount of space for the dataset equal to the volume size. (If you look ahead to Chapter 6, it establishes a refreservation of equal size.) Changing **volsize** changes the reservation. The **volsize** can only be set to a multiple of the **volblocksize** property, and cannot be zero.

Without the reservation, the volume could run out of space, resulting in undefined behavior or data corruption, depending on how the volume is used. These effects can also occur when the volume size is changed while it is in use, particularly when shrinking the size. Adjusting the volume size can confuse applications using the block device.

Zvols also support *sparse volumes*, also known as *thin provisioning*. A sparse volume is a volume where the reservation is less than the volume size. Essentially, using a sparse volume permits allocating more space than the dataset has available. With sparse provisioning you could, say, create ten 1 TB sparse volumes on your 5 TB dataset. So long as your volumes are never heavily used, nobody will notice that you're overcommitted.

Sparse volumes are not recommended. Writes to a sparse volume can fail with an "out of space" error even if the volume itself looks only partially full.

Specify a sparse volume at creation time by specifying the -s option to the zfs create -V command. Changes to **volsize** are not reflected in the reservation. You can also reduce the reservation after the volume has been created.

Zvol Mode

FreeBSD normally exposes zvols to the operating system as geom(4) providers, giving them maximum flexibility. You can change this with the **volmode** property.

Setting a volume's **volmode** to *dev* exposes volumes only as a character device in /dev. Such volumes can be accessed only as raw disk device files. They cannot be partitioned or mounted, and they cannot participate in RAIDs or other GEOM features. They are faster. In some cases where you don't trust the device using the volume, dev mode can be safer.

Setting **volmode** to *none* means that the volume is not exposed outside ZFS. These volumes can be snapshotted, cloned, and replicated, however. These volumes can be suitable for backup purposes.

Setting `volmode` to *default* means that volume exposure is controlled by the sysctl vfs.zfs.vol.mode. You can set the default zvol mode system-wide. A value of *1* means the default is geom, *2* means dev, and *3* means none.

While you can change the property on a live volume, it has no effect. This property is processed only during volume creation and pool import. You can recreate the zvol device by renaming the volume with `zfs rename`.

Dataset Integrity

Most of ZFS' protections work at the VDEV layer. That's where blocks and disks go bad, after all. Some hardware limits pool redundancy, however. Very few laptops have enough hard drives to use mirroring, let alone RAID-Z. You can do some things at the dataset layer to offer some redundancy, however, by using checksums, metadata redundancy, and copies. Most users should never touch the first two, and users with redundant virtual devices probably want to leave all three alone.

Checksums

ZFS computes and stores checksums for every block that it writes. This ensures that when a block is read back, ZFS can verify that it is the same as when it was written, and has not been silently corrupted in one way or another. The `checksum` property controls which checksum algorithm the dataset uses. Valid settings are *on*, *fletcher2*, *fletcher4*, *sha256*, *off*, and *noparity*.

The default value, *on*, uses the algorithm selected by the OpenZFS developers. In 2015 that algorithm is *fletcher4*, but it might change in future releases.

The standard algorithm, *fletcher4*, is the default checksum algorithm. It's good enough for most use and is very fast. If you want to use *fletcher4* forever and ever, you could set this property to *fletcher4*. We recommend keeping the default of *on*, however, and letting ZFS upgrade your pool's checksum algorithm when it's time.

The value *off* disables integrity checking on user data.

The value *noparity* not only disables integrity but also disables maintaining parity for user data. This setting is used internally by a dump device residing on a RAID-Z pool and should not be used by any other dataset. Disabling checksums is not recommended.

Older versions of ZFS used the *fletcher2* algorithm. While it's supported for older pools, it's certainly not encouraged.

The *sha256* algorithm is slower than *fletcher4*, but less likely to result in a collision. In most cases, a collision is not harmful. The *sha256* algorithm is frequently recommended when doing deduplication.

Copies

ZFS stores two or three copies of important metadata, and can give the same treatment to your important user data. The `copies` property tells ZFS how many copies of user data to keep. ZFS attempts to put those copies on different disks, or failing that, as far apart on the physical disk as possible, to help guard against hardware failure. When you increase the `copies` property, ZFS also increases the number of copies of the metadata for that dataset, to a maximum of three.

If your pool runs on two mirrored disks, and you set `copies` to 3, you'll have six copies of your data. One of them should survive your ill-advised use of `dd(1)` on the raw provider device or that plunge off the roof.

Increasing or decreasing copies only affects data written after the setting change. Changing `copies` from *1* to *2* doesn't suddenly create duplicate copies of all your data, as we see here. Create a 10 MB file of random data.

```
# dd if=/dev/random of=/lamb/random1 bs=1m count=10
10+0 records in
10+0 records out
10485760 bytes transferred in 0.144787 secs (72421935
bytes/sec)
# zfs set copies=2 mypool/lamb
```

Now every block is stored twice. If one of the copies becomes corrupt, ZFS can still read your file. It knows which of the blocks is corrupt because its checksums won't match. But look at the space use on the pool (the REFER space in the pool listing).

```
# zfs list mypool/lamb
NAME            USED   AVAIL   REFER   MOUNTPOINT
mypool/lamb   10.2M   13.7G   10.1M   /lamb
```

Only the 10 MB we wrote were used. No extra copy was made of this file, as you wrote it before changing the copies property.

With copies set to 2, however, if we either write another file or overwrite the original file, we'll see different disk usage.

```
# dd if=/dev/random of=/lamb/random2 bs=1m count=10
10+0 records in
10+0 records out
10485760 bytes transferred in 0.141795 secs (73950181
  bytes/sec)
```

Look at disk usage now.

```
# zfs list mypool/lamb
NAME            USED   AVAIL   REFER   MOUNTPOINT
mypool/lamb   30.2M   13.7G   30.1M   /lamb
```

The total space usage is 30 MB, 10 for the first file of random data, and 20 for 2 copies of the second 10 MB file.

When we look at the files with ls(1), they only show the actual size:

```
# ls -l /lamb/random*
-rw-r--r--  1 root  wheel  10485760 Apr  6 15:27 /lamb/random1
-rw-r--r--  1 root  wheel  10485760 Apr  6 15:29 /lamb/random2
```

If you really want to muck with your dataset's resilience, look at metadata redundancy.

Metadata Redundancy

Each dataset stores an extra copy of its internal metadata, so that if a single block is corrupted, the amount of user data lost is limited. This extra copy is in addition to any redundancy provided at the VDEV level (e.g., by mirroring or RAID-Z). It's also in addition to any extra copies specified by the `copies` property (below), up to a total of three copies.

The `redundant_metadata` property lets you decide how redundant you want your dataset metadata to be. Most users should never change this property.

When `redundant_metadata` is set to *all* (the default), ZFS stores an extra copy of all metadata. If a single on-disk block is corrupt, at worst a single block of user data can be lost.

When you set `redundant_metadata` to *most*, ZFS stores an extra copy of only most types of metadata. This can improve performance of random writes, because less metadata must be written. When only most metadata is redundant, at worst about 100 blocks of user data can be lost if a single on-disk block is corrupt. The exact behavior of which metadata blocks are stored redundantly may change in future releases.

If you set `redundant_metadata` to *most* and copies to *3*, and the dataset lives on a mirrored pool, then ZFS stores six copies of most metadata, and four copies of data and some metadata.

This property was designed for specific use cases that frequently update metadata, such as databases. If the data is already protected by sufficiently strong fault tolerance, reducing the number of copies of the metadata that must be written each time the database changes can improve performance. Change this value only if you know what you are doing.

Now that you have a grip on datasets, let's talk about pool maintenance.

Chapter 5: Repairs & Renovations

Disks fill up. That's what they're for. Hardware fails for the same reason. Sometimes you must take disks from one machine and put them in another, or replace a failed hard drive, or give your database more space. This chapter discusses how you can modify, update, and repair your storage pools.

Before we get into that, let's discuss how ZFS rebuilds damaged virtual devices.

Resilvering

Virtual devices such as mirrors and RAID-Z are specifically designed to reconstruct missing data on damaged disks. If a disk in your mirror pair dies, you replace the disk and ZFS will copy the surviving mirror onto the new one. If a disk in your RAID-Z VDEV fails, you replace the broken drive and ZFS rebuilds that disk from parity data. This sort of data recovery is a core feature of every RAID implementation.

ZFS understands both the filesystem and the underlying storage, however. This gives ZFS latitude and advantages that traditional RAID managers lack.

Rebuilding a disk mirrored by software or hardware RAID requires copying every single sector from the good disk onto the replacement. The RAID unit must copy the partition table, the filesystem, all the inodes, all the blocks (even the free space), and all the data from one to the other.

We've all made a typo in /etc/rc.conf that prevented a system from booting. Fixing that typo on a system mirrored with UFS2 and gmirror(8) required booting into single-user mode, fixing the typo, and rebooting. This made one of the disks out of sync with the other. At the reboot, FreeBSD noticed the discrepancy and brought the backup disk into sync by copying every single sector of the current drive onto the backup. You might have changed one or two sectors on the disk, but gmirror(8) had to copy the whole thing. This might take hours or days.

ZFS knows precisely how much of each disk is in use. When ZFS reassembles a replacement storage provider, it copies only the data actually needed on that provider. If you replace a ZFS disk that was only one-third data, ZFS copies only that one-third of a disk of data to the replacement.

Fixing a rc.conf typo on a ZFS-mirrored disk requires sysadmin intervention very similar to that needed on a gmirror(8) system. You get into single-user mode. You fix the typo. You reboot. The difference is, ZFS knows exactly which blocks changed on the disk. If only one of the disks was powered on during single user mode (unlikely, but it could happen), the two disks would be out of sync. Rather than try to copy the entire disk, ZFS updates only the blocks needed to resynchronize the disks. The system will probably repair the mirror before you can type a command to see how it's doing.

ZFS reconstruction is called *resilvering*. Like other ZFS integrity operations, resilvering takes place only on live filesystems. You could resilver in single-user mode, but it makes as much sense as installing software in single-user mode.

Resilvering happens automatically when you replace a storage provider. It also happens when a drive temporarily fails and is restored, such as when a controller restarts or an external disk shelf reboots.

While resilvering a replacement storage provider can take quite a while, resilvering after a brief outage probably takes only seconds.

If you use a RAID-Z pool normally while resilvering, resilvering can greatly slow down. Resilvering and scrubbing are performed in order by transaction groups, while normal read-write operations are pretty random. ZFS' resilver rate is throttled so that it won't impact normal system function.

Expanding Pools

Data expands to fill all available space. No matter how much disk space you give a pool, eventually you'll want more. To increase a pool's size, add a VDEV to the pool. For redundant pools, you can replace storage providers with larger providers.

When you expand a pool, ZFS automatically starts writing data to the new space. As the pool ages, ZFS tries to evenly balance available space between the various providers. ZFS biases the writes to the drives so that they will all become full simultaneously. A pool with one empty VDEV and three nearly full ones has little choice but to put new data on the empty VDEV, however. If you frequently create and delete files, per-disk load eventually levels out.

Every VDEV within a zpool should be identical. If your pool is built from a bunch of mirrors, don't go adding a RAID-Z3 to the pool.

Add providers to VDEVs with the `zpool attach` command and VDEVs to pools with the `zpool add` command.

You can't remove a device from a non-mirror VDEV or any VDEV from a pool. The -n flag to `zpool add` performs a "dry run," showing you the results of what running the command would be without actually changing the pool. Running your `zpool add` command with the -n flag and carefully studying the resulting pool configuration can give you warning you're about to shoot yourself in the foot.

Adding VDEVs to Striped Pools

Striped pools, with no redundancy, can be expanded up to the limits of the hardware. Each non-redundant VDEV you add to a pool increases the odds of a catastrophic failure, however, exactly like the RAID-0 device it resembles. Remember, the failure of a single VDEV in a pool destroys the entire pool. In a striped pool, each disk is a standalone VDEV.

Here's a striped pool with three providers.

```
# zpool status scratch
...
config:

NAME          STATE   READ  WRITE  CKSUM
scratch       ONLINE  0     0      0
 gpt/zfs0     ONLINE  0     0      0
 gpt/zfs1     ONLINE  0     0      0
 gpt/zfs2     ONLINE  0     0      0
```

Use the `zpool add` command to add a storage provider to the scratch pool.

```
# zpool add scratch gpt/zfs3
```

The pool status now shows four storage providers, and you have your additional disk space.

Adding VDEVs to Striped Mirror Pools

You can add providers to a mirrored VDEV, but extra disks don't increase the available space. They become additional mirrors of each other. To add space to a pool that uses mirrored VDEVs, add a new mirror VDEV to the pool.

The zpool *db* currently has two mirror VDEVs in it.

```
# zpool status db
...
NAME             STATE    READ   WRITE   CKSUM
db               ONLINE    0       0        0
 mirror-0        ONLINE    0       0        0
   gpt/zfs0      ONLINE    0       0        0
   gpt/zfs1      ONLINE    0       0        0
 mirror-1        ONLINE    0       0        0
   gpt/zfs2      ONLINE    0       0        0
   gpt/zfs3      ONLINE    0       0        0
```

We need more space, so we want to add a third mirror VDEV. Use the `zpool add` command to create a new mirror device and add it to the pool. Here we use the providers *gpt/zfs4* and *gpt/zfs5* to create a new mirror and add it to the pool.

```
# zpool add db mirror gpt/zfs4 gpt/zfs5
```

The pool's status now shows a new mirror VDEV, mirror-2, containing two storage providers. As you write and delete data, the pool gradually shifts load among all three VDEVs. To view how a pool currently distributes data between the VDEVs, use `zpool list -v`.

Adding VDEVs to Striped RAID-Z Pools

You cannot add providers to any RAID-Z VDEV. To expand a RAID-Z-based pool, you must add additional VDEVs to the pool, or replace each member disk with a larger one. Best practice is to make all of the RAID-Z VDEVs use the same number of drives.

Here's a RAID-Z pool that we want to expand with another VDEV.

```
NAME             STATE    READ   WRITE   CKSUM
db               ONLINE    0       0        0
 raidz1-0        ONLINE    0       0        0
   gpt/zfs0      ONLINE    0       0        0
   gpt/zfs1      ONLINE    0       0        0
   gpt/zfs2      ONLINE    0       0        0
```

Again, we use the `zpool add` command to create a new VDEV and add it to the pool.

```
# zpool add db raidz1 gpt/zfs3 gpt/zfs4 gpt/zfs5
```

A check of the pool status shows a new VDEV, raidz1-1, containing three providers. ZFS starts striping data across the new provider immediately.

If you want to add a new VDEV to a RAID-Z2 or RAID-Z3-based pool, use the same command with the desired RAID-Z type and the appropriate number of providers.

Remember, you cannot add providers to a RAID-Z VDEV—the configuration of a RAID-Z VDEV is fixed in concrete. Many people try to add a disk to a RAID-Z VDEV by using `zpool add`. The `zpool add` command adds new VDEVs to a pool. If you use -f to demand `zpool add` put one new disk in your RAID-Z-based pool, you get a malformed pool with one RAID-Z member and one stripe member. The resulting pool is not maintainable and is irreparable. Fixing it requires backing up your data, then destroying and recreating the pool.

You can use `zpool attach` to expand mirrored and striped VDEVs, but it doesn't work on RAID-Z pools. You cannot add providers to a RAID-Z VDEV.

Hardware Status

Most ZFS configurations tolerate a certain amount of hardware failure. When the underlying storage providers fail, ZFS does its best to warn you. Listen to it.

The `zpool status` command displays the condition of the storage hardware in the STATE field. You get one STATE field for the entire pool, near the top. Lower down, where `zpool status` lists each VDEV and storage provider, the STATE column lets you narrow down where a fault lies.

Errors percolate upwards. If a single storage provider fails, the pool develops a related failure. The big screaming failure message at the top of `zpool status` is your clue to look into the individual providers to see the underlying error.

Pools and VDEVs can have six states. Underlying providers can have at least three of these states.

Online

An *online* pool, VDEV, or provider is working normally.

Degraded

A *degraded* pool is missing at least one storage provider. That provider is either totally offline, missing, or generating errors more quickly than ZFS tolerates. A degraded pool retains enough resiliency to continue working, but one more failure might shut it down.

If a storage provider has too many I/O errors, ZFS would prefer to totally shut down (fault) the device. ZFS really tries to avoid faulting devices that provide necessary resiliency to a pool, however. If the last working provider in a mirror starts showing many errors, or a provider fails in a RAID-Z1 VDEV that already has a dead storage provider, ZFS puts that provider into degraded mode when it would normally put it in a faulted mode.

Faulted

Faulted storage providers are either corrupt or generate more errors than ZFS can tolerate. A faulted storage provider takes with it the last known good copy of the data. If your two-disk mirror loses both disks, or your RAID-Z1 loses two disks, the VDEV faults. A faulted VDEV takes its whole pool with it.

Unavail

Unavail means that ZFS can't open the storage provider. Maybe the device isn't attached to the system anymore, or perhaps it was badly imported (see "Moving Pools" later this chapter). In any case, it's not there, so ZFS can't use it. An unavailable device might take the whole VDEV, and hence the whole pool, with it.

An unavailable device impacts the VDEV's state depending on the resiliency in the VDEV. If a pool still has enough resilience to function, the pool becomes degraded. If the VDEV can no longer function, it faults.

Unavailable devices appear in the pool's status by the GUID assigned to them rather than the provider's device node.

Offline

Offline devices have been deliberately turned off by the sysadmin. You have no end of reasons for turning off a drive in a large array.

Removed

Some hardware can detect when a drive is physically removed from the system while the system is running. Such hardware lets ZFS set the *Removed* status when a drive is pulled. When you reattach the drive, ZFS tries to bring the provider back online.

Errors through the ZFS Stack

Here's a server with a couple disconnected storage providers. This doesn't belong to Lucas' or Jude's system; it belongs to Lucas' friend's system.[12] Note the errors on the providers, the type of VDEV, and the state of the pool as a whole.

---

12   And now that Lucas has a good example of a problem, he can tell that friend that this zpool is wounded. Although, to be certain he has good examples, he'll probably wait until he finishes this book. Being Lucas' friend kind of sucks.

```
# zpool status
  pool: FreeNAS02
 state: DEGRADED
status: One or more devices could not be opened.  Sufficient replicas
        exist for the pool to continue functioning in a degraded
        state.
action: Attach the missing device and online it using 'zpool online'.
   see: http://illumos.org/msg/ZFS-8000-2Q
  scan: scrub repaired 0 in 15h57m with 0 errors on Sun Feb  8
15:57:55 2015
config:

NAME                 STATE      READ    WRITE   CKSUM
FreeNAS02            DEGRADED      0        0       0
  raidz2-0          DEGRADED      0        0       0
    15881943619...  UNAVAIL       0        0       0   was /dev/gpt/zfs0
    gpt/zfs1        ONLINE        0        0       0
    gpt/zfs2        ONLINE        0        0       0
    gpt/zfs3        ONLINE        0        0       0
    gpt/zfs4        ONLINE        0        0       0
    gpt/zfs5        ONLINE        0        0       0
    gpt/zfs6        ONLINE        0        0       0
    gpt/zfs7        ONLINE        0        0       0
    gpt/zfs8        ONLINE        0        0       0
    gpt/zfs9        ONLINE        0        0       0
    14768132704...  UNAVAIL       0        0       0   was /dev/gpt/zfs10
    gpt/zfs11       ONLINE        0        0       0
    gpt/zfs12       ONLINE        0        0       0
    gpt/zfs13       ONLINE        0        0       0
```

This RAID-Z2 pool is in a degraded state. It's missing two providers, /dev/gpt/zfs0 and /dev/gpt/zfs10. A RAID-Z2 VDEV can handle up to two disk failures, and will continue to function despite the missing drives.

A degraded pool has limited self-healing abilities, however. A pool without redundancy does not have the information necessary for ZFS to repair files. Our sample pool above has lost two disks out of its RAID-Z2 VDEV. It has zero redundancy. If a file suffers from bit rot, ZFS can't fix it. When you try to access that file, ZFS returns an error. Redundancy at the dataset layer (with the **copies** property) might let ZFS heal the file.

If this pool experiences another drive failure, the pool will no longer have a complete copy of its data and will fault.

111

Restoring Devices

If ZFS is kind enough to announce its problems, the least you can do is try to fix them. The repair process depends on whether the drive is missing or failed.

Missing Drives

A drive disconnected during operation shows up as either removed or faulted. Maybe you removed a drive to check its serial number. Perhaps a cable came loose. It might have been gremlins. In any case, you probably want to plug it back in.

If the hardware notices that the drive is removed, rather than just saying it's missing, the hardware also notices when the drive returns. ZFS attempts to reactivate restored drives.

Hardware that doesn't notify the operating system when drives are added or removed needs sysadmin intervention to restore service. Use the `zfs online` command to bring a reconnected drive back into service.

```
# zfs online gpt/zfs5
```

If the drive is offline because it's failed, though, you must replace it rather than just turn it back on.

Replacing Drives

The hardest part of drive replacement often has nothing to do with ZFS: you must find the bad drive. We advise using the physical location of the disk in the GPT label for the disk when you first install the drive to make later replacement easier. If you must identify a failed drive without this information, use `gpart list` and `smartctl` to get the disk's serial number and manufacturer, then search the chassis for that drive. It's the same process discussed in Chapter 0, in reverse, with the added pressure of unscheduled downtime. Worst case, you can find the serial number of every drive that is still working, and process of elimination will reveal which drive is missing.

Now don't you wish you'd done the work in advance?

Once you find the failed drive and arrange its replacement, that's where we can start to use ZFS.

Faulted Drives

Use the command `zpool replace` to remove a drive from a resilient VDEV and swap a new drive in. The drive doesn't have to be failed—it could be a perfectly healthy drive that you want to replace so that you can, say, do maintenance on the disk shelf. Here's a RAID-Z1 pool with a bad drive.

```
NAME               STATE    READ  WRITE   CKSUM
db                 DEGRADED    0      0       0
 raidz1-0          DEGRADED    0      0       0
  gpt/zfs1         ONLINE      0      0       0
  gpt/zfs2         ONLINE      0      0       0
  gpt/zfs3         FAULTED     0      0       0
  gpt/zfs4         ONLINE      0      0       0
```

The */var/log/messages* log includes many warnings about the physical disk underlying *gpt/zfs3*. This disk needs to be put out of our misery. Use `zpool replace` to remove the faulted provider from the VDEV and replace it with a new device. Give the pool name, the failed provider, and the new provider.

zpool replace db gpt/zfs3 gpt/zfs5

This command might take a long time, depending on the disk's capacity and speed and the amount of data on the disk. You can view the status of the replacement by checking the pool's status.

```
# zpool status db
  pool: db
 state: DEGRADED
status: One or more devices is currently being
        resilvered.  The pool will continue to
        function, possibly in a degraded state.
action: Wait for the resilver to complete.
  scan: resilver in progress since Mon Mar 16
        12:04:50 2015
        195M scanned out of 254M at 19.5M/s, 0h0m to go
        47.3M resilvered, 76.56% done
config:

NAME             STATE    READ  WRITE  CKSUM
db               ONLINE    0     0      0
 raidz1-0        ONLINE    0     0      0
  gpt/zfs1       ONLINE    0     0      0
  gpt/zfs2       ONLINE    0     0      0
  replacing-2    ONLINE    0     0      0
  gpt/zfs3       FAULTED   0     0      0
  gpt/zfs5       ONLINE    0     0      0   (resilvering)
  gpt/zfs4       ONLINE    0     0      0
```

The resilvering time estimates given assume that disk activity is fairly constant. Starting a big database dump halfway through the resilvering process delays everything.

Replacing the Same Slot

Perhaps your hard drive array is full, and you don't have the space to slot in a new hard drive with a new device node. You must physically remove the failed hard drive, mount the replacement in its space, partition and label the drive, and replace the provider. That's only slightly more complex.

This method has more risks, however. With zpool replace, the faulted provider remains as online as it can manage until resilvering finishes. If you lose a second disk in your RAID-Z1 during resilvering, there's a chance the pool has enough data integrity to survive. If you replace the faulty provider before starting the rebuild, you lose that safety line. If your hardware doesn't give you the flexibility you need for a safer replacement, though, check your backups and proceed.

Start by taking the failed provider offline. This tells ZFS to stop trying to read or write to the device.

```
# zpool offline gpt/zfs3
```

You can now remove the failed drive from the array and install its replacement. Partition the provider as needed. If you're unsure of partitioning, you can copy an existing disk's partition table to another disk with something like `gpart backup da0 | gpart restore da9`. Use the new provider label in `zpool replace`. If the label on the new provider is identical to the label on the drive you removed, you don't have to repeat the provider name. Here we replace `gpt/zfs3` with a new disk, also labeled `gpt/zfs3`.

```
# zpool replace db gpt/zfs3
```

If you're labeling your disks by serial number, as we recommend in Chapter 0, you won't have this issue.

Replacing Unavail Drives

If a drive status is UNAVAIL, ZFS identifies the missing drive by its GUID and gives the previous device name off to the side. The zpool can still function, but you really need to replace the drive.

```
NAME              STATE    READ  WRITE  CKSUM
db                DEGRADED    0      0      0
  RAID-Z1-0       DEGRADED    0      0      0
    gpt/zfs1      ONLINE      0      0      0
    gpt/zfs2      ONLINE      0      0      0
    137922168...  UNAVAIL     0      0      0   was /dev/gpt/zfs3
    gpt/zfs4      ONLINE      0      0      0
```

I've installed a new drive, which shows up in `/var/run/dmesg.boot` as da5, and created a freebsd-zfs partition on it. This new provider gets the GPT label zfs3. The pool won't automatically identify this

provider as its replacement—it knows that the previous provider was
/dev/gpt/zfs3, but the new */dev/gpt/zfs3* lacks the on-disk metadata
that identifies it as a ZFS volume.

To slip this new provider into the zpool, use `zpool replace` again.
Use the GUID instead of the previous device name.

```
# zpool replace db 13792229702739533691 gpt/zfs3
```

Checking the zpool's status shows the pool resilvering. Once the
resilver completes, the pool is fully restored.

Replacing Mirror Providers

Sometimes a disk doesn't totally fail, but generates so many errors that
it's clearly about to die. When this disk is in a mirrored virtual device,
it might be better to keep the failing provider in place while you add
the replacement disk. This maximizes redundancy throughout the
replacement process. It does require that your hardware be able to use
three disks instead of the usual two. If your system can handle only
two disks, then stick with `zpool replace`.

Here we have a pool with a single mirror VDEV containing
two providers, *gpt/zfs0* and *gpt/zfs1*. We must replace the dying
gpt/zfs0 with *gpt/zfs2*. Rather than going straight to `zpool replace`,
start by attaching the replacement disk to pool. The `zpool attach`
command tells this pool to add another layer of mirroring to the pool.
Give the pool name, a device to be mirrored, and the new device.

```
# zpool attach db gpt/zfs1 gpt/zfs2
```

Here we attach a provider to the pool *db*. One of the existing providers is *gpt/zfs1*, and we're attaching *gpt/zfs2*. Look at `zpool status`
db and you'll see the pool resilvering to synchronize the new provider
with the other disks in the mirror. Once the new provider is synchronized with the pool, remove the failing provider from the virtual
device.

```
# zpool detach db gpt/zfs0
```

The failing disk behind *gpt/zfs0* is no longer in use.

You can also use this technique to transform a single-disk pool into a mirrored virtual device.

Reattaching Unavail and Removed Drives

An UNAVAIL drive might not have catastrophically failed. It might have come unplugged. If you go to the server and find that wiggling the drive tray makes it light up, you can tell the zpool to reactivate the disk. You can also reactivate a drive with a status of REMOVED. In either case use the `zpool online` command, the pool name, and the GUID of the missing provider.

```
# zpool online db 718035988381613979
```

ZFS will resilver the reactivated drive and resume normal function.

Log and Cache Device Maintenance

We advise using high-endurance SSD drives for your ZFS Intent Log (write cache) and L2ARC (read cache). All too often you'll find that "high endurance" is not the same as "high enough endurance," and you might need to replace the device. Log devices use the same status keywords as regular storage providers—*faulted*, *offline*, and so on. You might also need to insert a log device or, less commonly, remove the log device.

While the examples show log devices, cache devices work exactly the same way.

Adding a Log or Cache Device

To add a log or cache device to an existing pool, use `zpool add`, the pool name, and the device type and providers. Here we add the log device *gpt/zlog0* to the pool db.

```
# zpool add db log gpt/zlog0
```

The pool immediately begins using the new log or cache device.

To add a mirrored log device, use the *mirror* keyword and the providers. Mirroring the ZIL provides redundancy for writes, helping guarantee that data written to disk survives a hardware failure. Here we mirror the devices *gpt/zlog0* and *gpt/zlog1* and tell the pool *db* to use the mirror as a log device.

```
# zpool add db log mirror gpt/zlog0 gpt/zlog1
```

Most often, a mirrored cache device isn't a good use of fast disk. ZFS handles the death of a cache device fairly well. Striping the cache across multiple devices reduces load on any single device and hence reduces the chance of failure.

Removing Log and Cache Devices

When you remove a log or cache device from a ZFS pool, ZFS stops writing new data to the log, clears out the buffer of data from the log, and releases the device.

To remove a standalone log or cache device, use `zpool remove`, the pool name, and the device name. We previously added the device *gpt/zlog0* as a log device for the pool *db*. Let's remove it.

```
# zpool remove db gpt/zlog0
```

Removing a mirrored log device is slightly more complex. You must know the mirror name before you can remove it. Look at the pool status.

```
# zpool status db
...
NAME            STATE   READ  WRITE  CKSUM
db              ONLINE    0     0      0
 mirror-0       ONLINE    0     0      0
  gpt/zfs0      ONLINE    0     0      0
  gpt/zfs1      ONLINE    0     0      0
 mirror-1       ONLINE    0     0      0
  gpt/zfs2      ONLINE    0     0      0
  gpt/zfs3      ONLINE    0     0      0
 logs
 mirror-2       ONLINE    0     0      0
  gpt/zlog0     ONLINE    0     0      0
  gpt/zlog1     ONLINE    0     0      0
```

The log device is called mirror-2. Remove it as you would a stand-alone device.

```
# zpool remove db mirror-2
```

The pool clears the log and removes the device from the pool.

Replacing Failed Log and Cache Devices

Replace a failed log or cache device, even a mirror member, exactly as you would any other failed devices. Here we replace the device *gpt/zlog0* with *gpt/zlog2*.

```
# zpool replace db gpt/zlog0 gpt/zlog2
```

The log device resilvers and carries on.

Exporting and Importing Drives

You can move ZFS filesystem drives between machines, even machines running different operating systems. You aren't restricted to similar architectures, either—ZFS even lets you move disks between different endian hardware! This offers an easy migration path between, say, Sparc OpenSolaris and FreeBSD. ZFS uses its own on-disk metadata to track the role of each provider in a pool, so you don't need to track drive order, device nodes, or any of the usual disk issues. Unplug your drives, throw them in a bag, drive across town, and plug them back in. Bringing a pool back online is called *importing*.

ZFS can run on storage providers other than disks, however. Suppose you use GPT disk partitions on your ZFS disks, as we recommend. You might then decide to move those disks from your FreeBSD host to another operating system or another hardware architecture. If the new operating system or hardware doesn't recognize GPT partitions, the new host won't be able to find the pools to import them!

Before you import a pool, though, you must export it.

Exporting Pools

Export is roughly analogous to cleanly unmounting a traditional filesystem. ZFS marks the providers as inactive and completes all pending transactions. If you have a ZFS Intent Log (Chapter 2), the log is purged. Everything is written to the provider, the filesystem is unmounted, and the system is notified that these providers are now free for reuse.

Use `zpool export` and the pool name to export a pool. Here, we export the pool *db*.

```
# zpool export db
```

This command should run silently. Run `zpool list` to verify the pool is no longer on the system.

The system will refuse to export an active filesystem. Shut down any daemons writing to the dataset and change your shell's working directory away from the dataset. Stop tailing files. You can use `fstat(1)` or `lsof(8)` to identify processes using filesystems on that dataset.

Importing Pools

To see inactive pools attached to a system, run `zpool import`. This doesn't actually import any pools, but only shows what's available for import.

```
# zpool import
   pool: db
 id: 8407636206040904802
  state: ONLINE
 action: The pool can be imported using its name or
         numeric identifier.
 config:

db                ONLINE
 raidz1-0         ONLINE
  gpt/zfs1        ONLINE
  gpt/zfs2        ONLINE
  gpt/zfs3        ONLINE
  gpt/zfs4        ONLINE
```

This shows that the pool *db*, also known by a long numerical identifier, can be imported. You see the pool configuration at the bottom exactly as you would for an active pool.

The status ONLINE does not mean that the pool is active, but rather that the providers are all ready for use. As far as ZFS knows, this pool is ready to go.

Import the pool with `zpool import` and the pool name or numerical ID.

```
# zpool import db
```

If you have multiple inactive pools with the same name, import the pool by ID number instead.

```
# zpool import 8407636206040904802
```

You cannot import a pool if a pool of that name already exists, unless you rename the pool.

Renaming Imported Pools

Some of us reuse pool names between machines. When Lucas needs a dedicated pool for a database he always calls it *db*, because it's short and he's lazy. This is great for standardization—everyone knows exactly where the database files live. It's an annoyance when moving disks to another machine, though. Each machine can have only one pool of each name.

121

ZFS lets you permanently rename a pool by giving the new name after the existing name. Here we import the pool called *db* under the name *olddb*.

```
# zpool import db olddb
```

Datasets from the imported pool can be found in */olddb*. These renames are permanent. You can export and reimport the pool with its new name forever.

To temporarily mount a pool at a location other than its usual mount point, use the -R flag and an alternate root path.

```
# zpool import -R /dunno data
```

This temporarily adds the path */dunno* to all datasets in the imported pool. Exporting the pool removes the extra path and unsets the **altroot** property.

Use the **altroot** property when you don't know what's in a pool and you don't want to chance overlaying it on your existing datasets or filesystems. Remember, BSD filesystems are stackable! You can also use it in an alternate boot environment, where the imported pool might overlay the running root filesystem and hide the tools you need to manage the pool.

Incomplete Pools

You can't import a pool if it doesn't have enough members to provide all the needed data. Much as you can't use a RAID-Z1 if it's missing two disks, you can't import a RAID-Z1 with more than one missing disk.

```
# zpool import
   pool: db
 id: 8407636206040904802
  state: UNAVAIL
 status: One or more devices are missing from the
         system.
 action: The pool cannot be imported. Attach the missing
         devices and try again.
    see: http://illumos.org/msg/ZFS-8000-3C
 config:

db                         UNAVAIL    insufficient replicas
  RAID-Z1-0                UNAVAIL    insufficient replicas
   gpt/zfs1                ONLINE
   4300284214136283306     UNAVAIL    cannot open
   gpt/zfs3                ONLINE
   3061272315720693424     UNAVAIL    cannot open
```

This is a four-provider RAID-Z1, but two of the providers are missing. Check that the reinstalled disks are all correctly attached and try again.

Special Imports

Pool imports are highly useful in recovering from damaged systems. ZFS lets you work around many errors and problems when importing pools. This section takes you through some special cases of imports.

Destroying a pool doesn't actually destroy any data. It marks the pools as destroyed, but the pools and all their metadata remain on the hard drives until overwritten. To tell ZFS to search for destroyed but importable pools, add the -D flag.

```
# zpool import -D
```

The pool's status will show up as ONLINE (DESTROYED). The ONLINE means that the pool has everything it needs to function. Use the -D flag and the pool name or ID number to resurrect it.

```
# zpool import -D 8407636206040904802
```

If a pool is missing too many storage providers, you cannot import it. You cannot zpool online detached drives. Check the drive trays and make sure the drives you want to import are attached and powered on. The next time you run `zpool import`, reconnected drives will show up.

If a pool is missing its log device, add the -m flag to import it without that device. An exported pool should have everything on the storage providers.

```
# zpool import -m db
```

You can set pool properties when you import, by using the -o flag. Here we import and rename a database pool, and also make it read-only.

```
# zpool import -o readonly=on db olddb
```

We can now copy files from the old pool without damaging the pristine copy of the data.

You might want to import a damaged pool, to try to recover some part of the data on it. The -F flag tells `zpool import` to roll back the last few transactions. This might return the pool to an importable state. You'll lose the contents of the rolled back transactions, but if this works, those transactions were probably causing your problems anyway.

Larger Providers

One interesting fact about ZFS is that it permits replacing providers with larger providers. If your redundant storage pool uses 4 TB disks you can replace them with, say, 10 TB models and increase the size of your pool. This requires replacing successive providers with larger ones.

A pool calculates its size by the smallest disk in each VDEV. If your mirror has a 4 TB disk and a 10 TB disk in a single VDEV, the mirror VDEV will only have 4 TB of space. There's no sensible way to mirror 10 TB of data on a 4 TB disk! If you replace the 4 TB disk, however, you'll be able to expand the mirror to the size of the smallest disk.

One question to ask is: do you want your pools to automatically expand when they can, or do you want to manually activate the expansion? ZFS can automatically make the expansion work, but you need to set the **autoexpand** property for each pool before starting. ZFS leaves this off by default because you can never shrink a pool. (Having to turn on **autoexpand** won't hurt you, but having it on by default might leave you with a pool too large for any of your other disks.)

```
# zpool set autoexpand=on db
```

Without this property set, you must run a command to expand the pool after you replace the providers.

Replacing all the providers in a pool isn't complicated, but it does involve a certain amount of tediousness. Take this RAID-Z1 pool with three providers.

```
NAME           STATE  READ   WRITE   CKSUM
db             ONLINE   0      0       0
 raidz1-0      ONLINE   0      0       0
  gpt/zfs1     ONLINE   0      0       0
  gpt/zfs2     ONLINE   0      0       0
  gpt/zfs3     ONLINE   0      0       0
```

Each of those providers is a single tiny disk.

```
# zpool list db
NAME  SIZE   ALLOC   FREE    FRAG  EXPANDSZ  CAP  DEDUP  HEALTH  ALTROOT
db    59.5G  1.43G   58.1G   1%        -      2%  1.00x  ONLINE  -
```

If the hardware has enough physical space, add new drives and create replacement providers. If you're short on physical space, offline the providers and replace the hard drives. Here we offline and replace the drives.

This pool has three providers: *gpt/zfs1*, *gpt/zfs2*, and *gpt/zfs3*. We first replace *gpt/zfs1*. Running gpart show -l shows that this provider is on drive da1.

If you need to offline the drive to add the replacement drive, start by identifying the physical location of drive da1. Prepare the replacement drive as required by your hardware, then offline the pool from the provider.

```
# zpool offline db gpt/zfs1
```

This should return silently. Checking `zpool status` shows this provider is offline. You can remove this hard drive from the system.

Insert the replacement drive, either in the space where the old drive was removed or a new slot. The new drive should appear in `/var/run/dmesg.boot`. On this system, the new drive shows up as `/dev/da4`. Create the desired partitioning on that drive and label it. If you're not using serial numbers in your labels, but labeling only by physical location, you can use the same label. (Again, we use these short labels here because they're easier to read while learning.)

```
# gpart create -s gpt da4
da4 created
# gpart add -a 1m -t freebsd-zfs -l zfs1 da4
```

Now tell the pool to replace the failed device.

```
# zpool replace -f db gpt/zfs1
```

Let the pool finish resilvering before replacing any other providers. Replacing a non-redundant unit during a resilvering will only cause pain. If you're using RAID-Z2 or RAID-Z3 it is possible to replace multiple disks simultaneously, but it's risky. An additional disk failure might make the VDEV fail. Without the redundancy provided by the additional providers, ZFS cannot heal itself. Each disk's I/O limits will probably throttle resilvering speed.

After your first provider resilvers, swap out your next smaller provider. You will see no change in disk space until you swap out every provider in the VDEV. To be sure you've replaced every providers with a larger one, check `zpool list`.

```
# zpool list db
NAME  SIZE  ALLOC   FREE   FRAG  EXPANDSZ  CAP  DEDUP  HEALTH  ALTROOT
db    59.5G  1.70G  57.8G   0%      240G    2%  1.00x  ONLINE  -
```

Note that we now have new space in EXPANDSZ. This pool can be grown.

If you set the pool to autoexpand before you started, it should grow on its own. If not, manually expand each device in the pool with `zpool online -e`.

```
# zpool online -e db gpt/zfs1
# zpool online -e db gpt/zfs2
# zpool online -e db gpt/zfs3
```

This pool now has more space.

Zpool Versions and Upgrades

The FreeBSD and OpenZFS teams constantly improve their software, adding new features to ZFS and to FreeBSD's ZFS support. Some of these improvements require changes or additions to the zpools. When you upgrade your host's operating system, the host might gain ZFS features that the existing pools don't support. Before you can use those new features, you must upgrade the storage pools. Pools continue to function if you don't upgrade them, but they won't take advantage of new features that require on-disk format changes.

You might choose to not upgrade your pools when you upgrade your operating system, however. If you're upgrading a system from FreeBSD 11 to FreeBSD 12, you might leave the disks in the pool format for FreeBSD 11. If you need to roll back the upgrade, the operating system will still be able to read the pools. Operating system upgrades are reversible. Pool upgrades are not.

ZFS Versions and Feature Flags

Originally, ZFS used version numbers to indicate which features a pool or operating system version supported. Version numbers started at 1 and increased by one for every ZFS improvement that touched the on-disk format. When Sun Microsystems acted as the central coordinator of all ZFS development, a single incrementing version number made sense. The version number in OpenZFS is set to 5000, and pools use feature flags instead. We discuss feature flags in detail in Chapter 3.

The two questions for feature flags are: "What features does your pool currently support?" and "What features does your operating system support?" Check the pool properties to see what's on your disks, as discussed in Chapter 3. To see all the feature flags your FreeBSD release supports, run `zpool upgrade -v`.

```
# zpool upgrade -v
This system supports ZFS pool feature flags.
The following features are supported:
FEAT DESCRIPTION
-------------------------------------------------------------
------
async_destroy                          (read-only compatible)
   Destroy filesystems asynchronously.
empty_bpobj                            (read-only compatible)
   Snapshots use less space.
lz4_compress
   LZ4 compression algorithm support.
...
```

The features marked "read-only compatible" mean that hosts that don't support these feature flags can import these pools, but only as read-only. See "Pool Import and Export" earlier this chapter for a discussion of moving pools between hosts.

The FreeBSD release notes for each version indicate new ZFS features. You do read the release notes carefully before upgrading, don't you? If you somehow miss that part of the documentation, `zpool` status tells you which pools could use an upgrade. (Remember, just because a pool can take an upgrade doesn't mean that you should do the upgrade. If you might need to revert an operating system upgrade, leave your pool features alone!)

```
# zpool status db
 pool:   db
state:   ONLINE
status: Some supported features are not enabled on the
         pool. The pool can still be used, but some fea-
         tures are unavailable.
action: Enable all features using 'zpool upgrade'. Once
         this is done, the pool may no longer be acces-
         sible by software that does not support the
         features. See zpool-features(7) for details.
...
```

You'll also get a list of the new features supported by the upgrade. Upgrade your pools by running zpool upgrade on the pool.

```
# zpool upgrade zroot
```

Pool upgrades non-reversibly add new fields to the existing pool layout. An upgrade doesn't rewrite existing data, however. While the new feature might have problems, the mere availability of that feature flag on the disk is very low risk.

If you plan to move disks to a system running an older operating system, or to an operating system running an older version of OpenZFS, you can enable pool features more selectively. Moving disks from a FreeBSD 11 system to a FreeBSD 10 system requires carefully checking pool features. Enable a single feature by setting its property to *enabled*.

```
# zpool set feature@large_blocks=enabled data
```

This pool now supports the large_blocks feature.

Zpool Upgrades and the Boot Loader

FreeBSD's boot loader must understand the ZFS pool you're booting from. This means it must recognize the pool's features. Any time you update the pool containing the */boot* filesystem, you must update the boot loader on the disks. Use gpart(8) to update the boot loader. If you boot from a ZFS mirror on the disks da0 and da1, you'll update the loaders on both disks like so:

```
# gpart bootcode -b /boot/pmbr -p /boot/gptzfsboot -i 1 da0
# gpart bootcode -b /boot/pmbr -p /boot/gptzfsboot -i 1 da1
```

The system might not boot without this update. The zpool upgrade command prints a reminder to perform the update, but you're free to ignore it if you like. If you render your system unbootable, you might try to boot from the newest FreeBSD-current ISO or a live CD and copy its boot loader to your system.

FreeBSD ZFS Pool Limitations

FreeBSD does not yet support all ZFS features. Most unsupported features don't work because of fundamental differences between the FreeBSD and Solaris architectures. People are actively developing solutions that will let FreeBSD support all of ZFS' features. We expect some of these to become supported after this book goes to press.

At this time, hot spares do not work. Hot spares let ZFS automatically swap a failed drive with an assigned standby on the system. This depends on the forthcoming zfsd(8) implementation, which is still a work in progress.

Now that you can fill a pool with data and repair the hardware, let's play with a couple of ZFS' more useful features, clones and snapshots.

Chapter 6: Disk Space Management

ZFS makes it easy to answer questions like "How much free disk does this pool have?" The question "What's using up all my space?" is much harder to answer thanks to snapshots, clones, reservations, ZVOLs, and referenced data. These features might also cause problems when trying to use traditional filesystem management methods on ZFS datasets. It's possible to find you don't have enough space to delete files, which is terribly confusing until you understand what's happening.

ZFS offers ways to improve disk space utilization. Rather than requiring the system administrator to compress individual files, ZFS can use compression at the filesystem level. ZFS can also perform deduplication of files, vastly improving disk usage at the cost of memory. We'll see how to evaluate these options and determine when to use each.

But let's start by considering ZFS' disk space usage.

Reading ZFS Disk Usage

The df(1) program shows the amount of free space on each partition, while du(1) shows how much disk is used in a partition or directory tree. For decades, sysadmins have used these tools to see what's eating their free space. They're great for traditional filesystems. ZFS requires different ways of thinking, however.

Consider this (heavily trimmed) list of ZFS datasets.

```
# zfs list
NAME                    USED  AVAIL  REFER  MOUNTPOINT
zroot                   17.5G  874G   144K  none
zroot/ROOT              1.35G  874G   144K  none
zroot/ROOT/default      1.35G  874G  1.35G  /
zroot/usr               12.5G  874G   454M  /usr
zroot/usr/local         1.84G  874G  1.84G  /usr/local
...
```

According to this, the *zroot* pool has 17.5 GB in use. At first glance you might think that *zroot/ROOT* and *zroot/ROOT/default* both use 1.35 GB. You'd be wrong.

The dataset *zroot/ROOT* uses 1.35 GB of data. There's 1.35 GB of data in this dataset. The dataset *zroot/ROOT/default* also uses 1.35 GB of data. The *zroot/ROOT/default* dataset is included in the *zroot/ROOT* dataset, however. It's the same 1.35 GB of data.

Similarly, consider the 12.5 GB that *zroot/usr* uses. This dataset has child datasets, such as *zroot/usr/local*, *zroot/usr/obj*, and so on. Each of these datasets uses a chunk of data, often several gigabytes. The 12.5 GB that *zroot/usr* uses includes everything beneath it.

With ZFS, you can't just add up the amount of used space to get the total.

The AVAIL column, or space available, is somewhat more reliable. The pool *zroot* has 874 GB of empty space. Once you start using snapshots and clones and all of the other ZFS goodness, you'll find that this 874 GB of space can contain many times that much data, thanks to referenced data.

Referenced Data

The amount of data included in a dataset is the referenced data. Look at the REFER column in the listing above. The *zroot* pool and *zroot/ROOT* both refer to 144 KB of space. That's roughly enough to say that "yes, this chunk of stuff exists." It's a placeholder. The dataset *zroot/ROOT/default*, however, references 1.35 GB of data.

The referenced data is stuff that exists within this filesystem or dataset. If you go into the *zroot/ROOT/default* filesystem, you'll find 1.35 GB of stuff.

So, you add up the referenced space and get the amount used? No, wrong again. Multiple ZFS datasets can refer to the same collection of data. That's exactly how snapshots and clones work. That's why ZFS can hold, for example, several 10 GB snapshots in 11 GB of space.

Clones use space much like snapshots, except in a more dynamic manner. Once you add in deduplication and compression, disk space usage gets complicated really quickly.

And then there are even issues around freeing space.

Freeing Space

In many ZFS deployments, deleting files doesn't actually free up space. In most situations, deletions actually increase disk space usage by a tiny amount, thanks to snapshots and metadata. The space used by those files gets assigned to the most recent snapshot. To successfully manage ZFS, you have to understand how the underlying features work and what ZFS does when you delete data.

On a filesystem using snapshots and clones, newly freed space doesn't appear immediately. Many ZFS operations free space asynchronously, as ZFS updates all the blocks that refer to that space. The pool's **freeing** property shows how much space ZFS still needs to reclaim from the pool. If you free up a whole bunch of space at once, you can watch the **freeing** property decrease and the free space increase. How quickly ZFS reclaims space depends on your hardware, the amount of load, pool design, fragmentation level, and how the space was used.

Asynchronously freeing space is easily understood: you look at the **freeing** property and see how quickly it goes down. But to the uninitiated, ZFS' disk use can seem much weirder. Suppose you have a bunch of dataset snapshots, and their parent dataset gets full. (We cover snapshots in Chapter 7, but bear with us now.) You delete a couple of large ISOs from the dataset. Deleting those files won't free up any space. Why not?

Those ISO files still exist in the older snapshots. ZFS knows that the files don't exist on the current dataset, but if you go look in the snapshot directories you'll see those files. ZFS must keep copies of those deleted files for the older snapshots as long as the snapshots refer to that data. Snapshots contents are read-only, so the only way to remove those large files is to remove the snapshots. If you have multiple snapshots, disk usage gets more complex. And clones (Chapter 7), built on snapshots, behave the same way.

Understanding precisely how a particular dataset uses disk space requires spending some time with its properties.

Disk Space Detail

To see exactly where your disk space went, ask `zfs list` for more detail on space usage with the `-o space` modifier.

```
# zfs list -o space
NAME                AVAIL   USED USEDSNAP  USEDDS USEDREFRESERV USEDCHILD
zroot               874G  17.5G        0    144K             0     17.5G
zroot/ROOT          874G  1.35G        0    144K             0     1.35G
zroot/ROOT/default  874G  1.35G        0   1.35G             0         0
zroot/usr           874G  12.5G        0    454M             0     12.0G
...
```

The AVAIL column shows the amount of space available to each of the datasets on this pool. ZFS shares the available space amongst all of the datasets in the pool. This is taken from the ZFS property **available**. We show how to limit usage with quotas and reservations later in this chapter.

134

The USED column shows the amount of space taken up by this dataset and everything descended from it. Snapshots, ZVOLs, clones, regular files, and anything else that uses space counts against this amount. This value might lag behind changes for a few seconds as ZFS writes new files, creates snapshots and child datasets, or makes other changes. The value comes from the dataset's `used` property.

The USEDBYSNAP column shows the amount of space used exclusively by snapshots. When you first snapshot a dataset, the snapshot takes almost no space, because it's nearly identical to the original dataset. As the dataset changes, however, the snapshots grow. As multiple snapshots of the same dataset probably refer to the same data, it's difficult to say if deleting a single snapshot will free up any part of this space. Completely removing all of this dataset's snapshots will certainly free up this amount of space, however. This value comes from the dataset's `usedbysnapshots` property. Chapter 7 discusses snapshots.

The USEDDS column shows the amount of space used by files on this dataset. It excludes snapshots, reservations, child datasets, or other special ZFS features. It comes from the dataset's `usedbydataset` property. Chapter 4 covers datasets.

Under USEDBYREFRESERV you'll see the space used by a refreservation for this dataset, excluding its children. This value comes from the dataset's `usedbyrefreserv` property. See "Reservations and Quotas" later in this chapter.

The USEDCHILD column shows how much space this dataset's children use, as shown by the `usedbychildren` property.

Compare the entry for *zroot/usr* in *zfs list* from the previous section to the detailed space description. The *zfs list* result says that the dataset uses 12.5 GB and refers to 454 MB. By breaking the space-specific list into different categories, it's very clear that this dataset uses 454 MB, and the child datasets take up 12 GB.

Use `zfs list -o space` whenever you investigate disk usage.

Pool Space Usage

Sometimes you don't care about the space usage of individual datasets. Only the space available to the pool as a whole matters. If you look at a pool's properties, you'll see properties that look an awful lot like the amount of space used and free. They are, but a pool's space properties include space required for parity information. They don't reflect the amount of data you can fit on the pool.

If you have a mirror or a striped pool, the pool space information is fairly close to reality. If you're using RAID-Z1, you'll lose one provider of space to parity per virtual device in the pool. RAID-Z2 costs two disks per VDEV, and RAID-Z3 costs three disks per VDEV. While you could, in theory, use these properties, the pool's current usage, and a bit of math to get a good guess as to how much space you're using, there's an easier way: ask `zfs(8)` about the pool's root dataset.

```
# zfs list zroot
NAME    USED   AVAIL  REFER  MOUNTPOINT
zroot   37.7G  854G   144K   none
```

This pool is using 37.7 GB and has 854 GB free.

ZFS, df(1), and Other Traditional Tools

So ZFS has all kinds of fancy abilities to slice and dice its display of disk usage. After decades of using df(1) to look at disk usage, many of us are loathe to change. When you're using ZFS, however, the venerable df(1) and many other tools are not merely less than optimal—they're actively incorrect and give wrong or confusing answers for ZFS. We're going to use df(1) as an example, but many other tools have similar problems.

Traditional filesystems consist of a single partition. That partition has a size, based on the number of blocks allocated on the underlying disk. The df(1) tool iterates over each mounted filesystem, and shows the size of the partition, how much of that space is currently used, and how much is remaining as free space.

Walking through the filesystems doesn't work for ZFS, because datasets are not filesystems. ZFS exposes each dataset to the operating system as if it were a separate filesystem. A dataset does not have a maximum size (unless it has a quota). While you can set upper and lower limits on the size of a dataset, all ZFS datasets have access to all of the available free space in the pool.

To offer some semblance of compatibility with the traditional df(1) tool, ZFS tells a little white lie. Since a ZFS dataset has no "size" in the traditional filesystem sense, it sums the used space, and the entire pool's available free space together, and presents that value as the "size" of the dataset.

Look at our example pools in the previous section. The zroot/ROOT/default dataset uses 1.35 GB of space, and has 874 GB free. The total size is 875.35 GB. Then look at the zroot/usr dataset. It has used 12.5 GB, and has 874 GB free, for a total of 886.5 GB.

Now check some actual df(1) output for these datasets.

```
# df -h
Filesystem          Size  Used  Avail Capacity  Mounted on
zroot/ROOT/default  875G  1.4G  874G        0%  /
zroot/usr           874G  454M  874G        0%  /usr
...
```

The root filesystem is 875 GB, and /usr is 874 GB, giving these two partitions a total of 1749 GB, with 1748 GB free. Pretty impressive for a 1 TB disk, isn't it? The "Capacity" column that showed what percentage of the filesystem is in use is similarly bogus.

As datasets grow larger, the amount of free space shrinks. According to df(1), the filesystem shrinks as space is used up, and grows when space is freed.

Tools like df(1), and most other monitoring tools intended for traditional filesystems, give incorrect answers. Beware of them! While they might seem fine for a quick check, continuing to use these tools further ingrains bad habits. Bad systems administration habits cause pain and outages. When monitoring a dataset's free space, make sure you are measuring the actual amount of free space, rather than the percentage used. If a traditional tool that shows "percent used" gives a meaningful result, it's only by accident. Your monitoring system needs ZFS-specific tools.

This behavior has interesting side effects when viewed with other tools meant for traditional filesystems. A ZFS dataset mounted via Samba on a Windows machine will show only a minuscule amount of space used, and the remaining amount of space in the pool as the free space. As the pool fills with data, Windows sees the drive shrink.

When using ZFS, develop the habit of managing it with accurate tools.

Limiting Dataset Size

ZFS' flexibility means that users and applications can use disk space if it's available. This is very valuable, especially on long-lived systems, but sometimes that's the exact behavior you don't want. You don't want datasets like /var/log expanding to fill your disk and, inversely, you want to be certain that critical datasets like your database get the space they need. If the main database runs out of space because Jude temporarily stashed his collection of illicit potted fern photos in his home directory, you'll have an unpleasant and unnecessary meeting.[13] That's where quotas and reservations come in.

---

13   On the plus side, you'll have an excuse to throw Jude under the bus. Metaphorically, if you prefer.

A *quota* dictates the maximum amount of space a dataset and all its descendants can use up. If you set a quota of 100 GB on the dataset mounted as */home*, the total amount of space used by */home* and all the datasets and snapshots beneath it cannot exceed 100 GB.

A *reservation* dictates an amount of space set aside for a dataset. To ensure that a database always has room to write its files, use a reservation to carve out an amount of disk space just for that dataset.

We'll discuss reservations first, then proceed to quotas.

Reservations

A reservation sets aside a chunk of disk space for a dataset and its children. The system will not allow other datasets to use that space. If a pool runs out of space, the reserved space will still be available for writes to that dataset.

Suppose we reserve 100 GB out of a 1 TB pool for */var/db*, where our database stuffs its data files. This dataset has about 50 GB of data in it. A log file runs amok, and fills the rest of the pool. We'll get errors from the other programs on the system saying that the disk is full— but the database program will still have free space in */var/db*. It might complain that it can't write program logs to */var/log/db*, but that's a separate issue.

ZFS manages reservations with two ZFS properties: **refreservation** and **reservation**. A refreservation affects the dataset's referenced data—that is, it excludes snapshots, clones, and other descendants. A reservation includes child datasets, snapshots, and so on. For an example, look at this snippet from zfs list.

```
# zfs list
NAME                  USED   AVAIL  REFER  MOUNTPOINT
zroot/usr             12.5G  874G   454M   /usr
zroot/usr/local       1.84G  874G   1.84G  /usr/local
zroot/usr/obj         6.89G  874G   6.89G  /usr/obj
zroot/usr/ports       1.97G  874G   816M   /usr/ports
...
```

The `zroot/usr` dataset is mounted as `/usr`. It "uses" 12.5 GB, including child datasets such as `/usr/local`, `/usr/obj`, and so on. It refers to only 454 MB, meaning that the amount of data on the main `zroot/usr` dataset is less than half a gigabyte.

If we set a reservation of 1 GB on `zroot/usr`, that's basically moot. The existing files in the child datasets far exceed that, and the odds of something non-catastrophic trimming those children down to less than 1 GB are negligible.

If we set a refreservation of 1 GB on `zroot/usr`, though, it only affects files on `zroot/usr`. The child datasets are excluded. The dataset is currently half full, so it would have space to write more files.

That's an extreme example, but somewhat artificial. Suppose you want to ensure that all of your users get at least 1 GB of disk space. Create a separate dataset for each user's home directory and assign each a reservation.

You might also nest reservations. Suppose you have two data-sets, `zroot/var/log` and `zroot/var/log/db`, the latter exclusively for your database server. You want to always have at least 10 GB for your database server logs, so you assign a reservation to `zroot/var/log/db`. Then you want 20 GB for generic server logs. If that 20 GB should include the database logs, use a reservation. If it should not include the database logs, use a refreservation.

A dataset might have both a reservation and a refreservation. You might say that the dataset `zroot/var/log/db` has a 10 GB refreservation for current log files, but set a much larger reservation so that you can take snapshots of the dataset and count their usage separately.

Attempting to violate a reservation generates an "out of space" error. When that error appears even though you know you still have free disk space, check your reservations. The datasets with reservations will show free space, but all others will be full.

Viewing Reservations

You can check the reservations and refreservations separately, but we prefer to get all reservation information at once. You can view the specific list of properties by running `zfs get -o reservation,refreservation,usedbyrefreservation`, but Lucas is too blasted lazy to type all that and he's the lead author, so this example uses `grep(1)`.

```
# zfs get all zroot/var/log/db | grep reserv
zroot/var/log/db   reservation              none    default
zroot/var/log/db   refreservation           none    default
zroot/var/log/db   usedbyrefreservation  0         -
```

This dataset has no reservation or refreservation set. Let's set some.

The **usedbyrefreservation** property shows how much space on this dataset would be freed if the **refreservation** was removed.

Setting and Removing Reservations

Set a reservation just like you would any other ZFS property. Here we set a **refreservation** on */var/log/db* and a reservation on */var/log*.

```
# zfs set refreservation=10G zroot/var/log/db
# zfs set reservation=20G zroot/var/log
```

No matter what, this host will now have 10 GB reserved for database logs and 20 GB for the log files, including the database directory. We used a **refreservation** for the database logs because we don't want snapshots counted against that reservation.

To remove a reservation, set it to *none*.

```
# zfs set reservation=none zroot/var/log
```

Other datasets can now use that space.

Quotas

A *quota* is a maximum amount of space that a dataset, user, or user group may use. All of these quotas are set on a per-dataset basis. We'll start with dataset quotas, then investigate user and group quotas.

Dataset Quotas

Use a quota when you want to set a maximum amount of space that a dataset can consume. For example, you might decide that `/tmp` can only use up to 10 GB, or `/home` can only take up 200 GB, or any other limit that makes sense to you.

Like reservations, ZFS uses two properties for quotas: `quota` and `refquota`. The `quota` property sets a maximum amount of space that a dataset and all its children can use. The `refquota` property establishes the maximum amount of space that the dataset can use, excluding its children. If you want a quota that excludes snapshots and child datasets, use the `refquota` property.

Why would you want to use a `refquota` instead of a `quota`? Suppose each user's home directory is its own dataset, and users cannot create snapshots. Most can't, and most of those who can don't know how. If you automatically create snapshots, as we demonstrate in Chapter 7, then the space used by snapshots will get charged to the user's account. A user who runs out of disk space might delete some files but discover that they haven't freed any space. It's probably not fair to charge a user for disk space that they don't control.[14]

---

[14]   Sysadmins who consider "being fair to users" outside their normal remit can use refquotas as a way of reducing exposure to user cooties.

Setting Quotas

To configure a quota on a dataset, assign the quota and/or refquota properties.

In the Reservations section we set aside 20 GB for the system logs in the *zroot/var/log* dataset, guaranteeing that the log would always have at least 20 GB of space. A more common issue is when logging runs amok and absorbs all available disk space, crashing the system. Your monitoring system should catch this error, but it also makes sense to establish a quota on the log dataset so that someone uncommenting */var/log/all.log* in */etc/syslog.conf* doesn't crash the box a day later.

Here we set a quota on *zroot/var/log*.

```
# zfs set quota=100G zroot/var/log
```

The log files can use no more than 100 GB, including snapshots, child datasets, and everything else.

You can separately limit the amount of referenced data with a *refquota*. This excludes child datasets and snapshots. Limiting both the size of the entire dataset and the dataset's referenced data can help you control the size of your snapshots. For example, setting a refquota of 10 GB and a quota of 100 GB would tell you that you could always have 10 snapshots even if the data completely changes. Similarly, if you want to exclude child datasets, use a refquota.

```
# zfs set refquota=50G zroot/var/log
# zfs set refquota=50G zroot/var/log/db
# zfs set quota=500G zroot/var/log
```

Here we have separate refquotas for two logging datasets, and a quota for both of the datasets together. If each dataset can reference up to 50 GB on its own, the 500 GB quota means that no matter how the data changes, you can have at least four snapshots of each.

Viewing Quotas

To see the quotas on a dataset, check the `quota` and `refquota` properties.

```
# zfs get all zroot/home | grep quota
zroot/home   quota      none   default
zroot/home   refquota   none   default
```

The `/home` directory has no quotas on it. Users may fill your hard drive to its limits.

Quotas change the dataset's maximum size and the free space in the dataset. This pool has several hundred gigabytes free, but `zfs list` on this dataset says otherwise.

```
# zfs list zroot/var/log
NAME            USED   AVAIL   REFER   MOUNTPOINT
zroot/var/log   25.0G  75.0G   5.01G   /var/log
```

The `zroot/var/log` dataset has 25 GB on it, and 75 GB free. ZFS knows that the dataset has a 100 GB quota on it, and it shows utilization appropriately. You've just simulated a traditional partition by setting a quota—but don't go running for `df(1)`! First, look at a child dataset of `zroot/var/log`.

```
# zfs list zroot/var/log/db
NAME               USED   AVAIL   REFER   MOUNTPOINT
zroot/var/log/db   20.0G  85.0G   10.0G   /var/log/db
```

ZFS knows that the parent dataset has a quota of 100 GB, and therefore also sets that maximum size on the child datasets. If `/var/log` has 75 GB free, and `/var/log/db` has 85 GB free, does that mean that these two partitions have (75 + 85 =) 160 GB of free space? No, because like free space in a pool, these two entries both refer to the same free space. The dataset `zroot/var/log/db` entry seems to have more free space because data in its parent dataset is not reflected in the child dataset's usage.

Exceeded Quotas

If a user or process attempts to write something that would make the dataset exceed its quota, it will get a quota error.

```
# cp script.sh testscript.sh
cp: testscript.sh: Disc quota exceeded
```

You'll need to free some space, but remember that snapshots might complicate that, as discussed in "Freeing Space" earlier in this chapter. If you've set both a quota and a refquota, the user might be able to delete files and free up space even though that increases the size of the filesystem's snapshots.

User and Group Quotas

User and group quotas control how much data a user or a group can write to a dataset. Like dataset quotas, user and group quotas are controlled on a per-dataset basis.

User and group quotas don't apply to child filesystems, snapshots, and clones. You must apply quotas to each individual dataset you want them to affect.

Viewing Space Used and Existing Quotas per Dataset

The zfs userspace command lets you see how much space is used by each user in a dataset. Here we examine the *zroot/home* dataset on our test system. A system with complicated datasets might need several minutes to run du(1), but zfs userspace finds all the files owned by each user nearly instantaneously.

```
# zfs userspace zroot/home
TYPE         NAME        USED   QUOTA
POSIX User   179        7.29M   none
POSIX User   mwlucas    1.16G   none
POSIX User   root        298M   none
```

The user **mwlucas** has 1.16 GB of files—unsurprising. The **root** user has 298 MB of files in */home*—somewhat surprising, but not shocking.

145

Somehow, though, user 179 has 7.29 MB of files in that dataset. This system has no user 179, which is why the user is shown by UID rather than username. A bit of digging shows that Lucas once used tar's -p argument when extracting a source code tarball, preserving the original file ownership.

None of these users have quotas.

The zfs groupspace command shows how much space files owned by each group use. For something more interesting, I'm checking the group ownerships on the *zroot/usr/local* dataset.

```
# zfs groupspace zroot/usr/local
TYPE            NAME            USED  QUOTA
POSIX Group     _tss           25.5K  none
POSIX Group     bin            93.5K  none
POSIX Group     kmem            128K  none
POSIX Group     messagebus      392K  none
POSIX Group     polkit          115K  none
POSIX Group     wheel          1.85G  none
```

If your server supports multiple groups, such as development teams, research groups, or devotees of different BSD variants, you can assign each group or user a quota to restrict their disk usage.

Assigning and Removing User and Group Quotas

Use the **userquota** and **groupquota** properties to assign user and group quotas. To specify the user or group the quota belongs to, give the property name, an @ sign, and the user or group name. Give the quota for the user **mwlucas**, for example, with userquota@mwlucas.

```
# zfs set userquota@mwlucas=1G zroot/home
```

The previous section showed that the **mwlucas** account had over a gigabyte of data in it. The **mwlucas** account is over quota, and that user gets an error whenever he tries to create a file.

```
$ touch test
touch: test: Disc quota exceeded
```

Similarly, assign a group quota with the `groupquota` property, an @ sign, and the group name.

```
# zfs set groupquota@staff=10G zroot/home
```

If a user has repeatedly abused shared directories like */tmp*, assign them a restrictive quota.

```
# zfs set userquota@mwlucas=10m zroot/tmp
```

This user can use features like SSH agent forwarding, but he can't extract huge tarballs and monopolize the shared temporary space.

To remove a quota, set the quota to *none*.

Viewing Individual Quotas

If you're interested in the quota set for a specific user or group, ask ZFS for that one property.

```
# zfs get userquota@mwlucas zroot/tmp
NAME         PROPERTY             VALUE        SOURCE
zroot/tmp    userquota@mwlucas    10M          local
```

Now you can let your teams squabble among themselves over their disk space usage, without taking up your precious time. Congratulations!

ZFS Compression

You can't increase the size of an existing disk, but you can change how your data uses that disk. For decades, sysadmins have compressed files to make them take up less space. We've written all kinds of shell scripts to run our preferred compression algorithm on the files we know can be safely compressed, and we're always looking for additional files that can be compressed to save space. And we all know about that previously unknown log file that expands until it fills the partition and trips an alarm.[15]

---

15   You don't monitor disk space usage? Well, an outage is merely a different sort of alarm.

ZFS takes away that problem by compressing files in real time, at the filesystem level. Those log files your daemon writes? ZFS can compress them as they're written, rendering all those scripts irrelevant. This also amortizes the cost of compression as the system compresses everything on an ongoing basis rather than in a 3 AM frenzy of disk thrashing.

Compression imposes costs, however. Compression and decompression require CPU time, so blindly enabling the tightest `gzip` compression everywhere can add another constraint on disk performance. Any performance losses are most often more than made up by the reduction in disk activity, however. ZFS includes compression algorithms specifically designed for filesystem use.

Enabling Compression

ZFS compression works on a per-dataset basis. You can enable compression for some datasets but not others.

Enable and disable compression with the **compression** property. Here we check the compression setting.

```
# zfs get compress zroot/usr
NAME        PROPERTY     VALUE SOURCE
zroot/usr   compression  off   default
```

Enable compression by setting the **compression** property. The default compression algorithm, LZJB, isn't the most effective algorithm ZFS offers. Use LZ4 compression in almost all cases. Here we enable LZ4 compression on all datasets on the *zroot* pool, but specify *gzip-9* on the zroot/var/cdr dataset.

```
# zfs set compress=lz4 zroot
# zfs set compress=gzip-9 zroot/var/cdr
```

ZFS compresses files when the files are written to disk. If you have a dataset full of text files, adding compression won't make them shrink. To reduce disk space used by files, you must rewrite all the files after enabling compression.

Compression Algorithms

ZFS supports several compression algorithms. The default, *LZJB*, was specifically designed for filesystem use. It can quickly compress and decompress blocks with a modest compression ratio. It's not the best compression algorithm for routine use, however.

The *LZ4* algorithm is a newer and faster filesystem-specific compression algorithm. It outperforms LZJB in all ways. Not all data is compressible, but LZ4 quickly detects incompressible files and doesn't try to compress them. When you enable compression for a dataset, use LZ4 unless you have a specific use case for gzip compression.

The *ZLE* algorithm compresses strings of zeroes in files. It's a minimal compression system, and isn't terribly useful for most files. LZ4 is far more effective than ZLE, even on files with many runs of zeroes.

For special cases, ZFS supports *gzip* compression. Gzip uses much more CPU time than LZ4, but can be more effective for some datasets. The additional CPU time gzip requires makes the filesystem slower, but for data that's not accessed frequently the disk space savings might be worthwhile.

Gzip has nine compression levels, from 1 (the fastest but least effective) to 9 (the slowest but most aggressive). Specify a gzip compression level with a dash and the level.

```
# zfs set compress=gzip-1 zroot/var/log
```

If you specify *gzip* without a level, ZFS uses the gzip default of level 6.

Compression Properties

Several properties offer insight into how well ZFS compresses your data.

The `compressratio` property shows how compression has affected this dataset and all its children, while the `refcompressratio` property allows you to see how compression has impacted this dataset's referenced data.

Datasets have two properties just for compression scenarios, `logicalreferenced` and `logicalused`. A dataset's referenced space includes the effects of compression, but the `logicalreferenced` property excludes compression.

Similarly, the `used` property shows the amount of space actually consumed on the dataset and all its children, while `logicalused` shows the amount of uncompressed data in the dataset.

When you study all of these together, you can get a good idea of how compression has impacted your data.

Choosing an Algorithm

How can you tell if your data can benefit from compression, or how different algorithms affect file size? Get some of your typical data files and test them. Use `du(1)` or `ls -ls` to see a file's actual size on the disk. In testing your own data, you'll want to use a whole bunch of different files of your actual data. For this example, Lucas used the Human Genome Project as downloaded from Project Gutenberg.

```
# du hgp.txt
280721  hgp.txt
```

Uncompressed, this file takes up 280,721 blocks, or about 274 MB.

Our test dataset is called *db*. We have no other data on this dataset, so we can accurately assess compression's impact on this particular file. Now that we know the test file's uncompressed size, enable compression and see what happens.

```
# zfs set compression=on db
```

This activates LZJB compression. Check the file size now.

```
# du hgp.txt
280721  hgp.txt
```

The file size hasn't changed, but we enabled compression. What's going on? Remember, compression, deduplication, and similar features work only on files written after the feature is enabled. We must remove the file and put it back.

```
# rm /db/*
# cp /home/mwl/hgp.txt /db
```

Wait a few seconds so that ZFS can write everything to disk, and see what happens.

```
# du /db/hgp.txt
139577  /db/hgp.txt
```

The file uses only 139,577 blocks, or about 136 MB. It's shrunk about in half, as the dataset properties show.

```
# zfs get compressratio,refcompressratio db
NAME   PROPERTY          VALUE   SOURCE
db     compressratio     2.01x   -
db     refcompressratio  2.01x   -
```

The refcompressratio equals the compressratio because we have only one chunk of data on this dataset and only one dataset on this pool. On more complex pools, the values will probably differ.

So, the default algorithm reduced the size by half. Let's try the more efficient *lz4*.

```
# zfs set compression=lz4 db
```

Recopy the file to trigger LZ4 compression, wait a few seconds for ZFS to do its accounting, and see what happens.

```
# du /db/hgp.txt
146076  /db/hgp.txt
```

LZ4 compresses this data to 142 MB. LZ4 is not as effective as LZJB on this particular file. That's not terribly shocking—different algorithms work differently on different data.

151

Would gzip improve things further?

```
# zfs set compress=gzip-1 db/text
```

Re-copy the test file to the dataset and check the disk usage.

```
# du /db/hgp.txt
74104    /db/hgp.txt
```

This data now uses about 72 MB, and the dataset now has a **compressratio** of 3.78. Gzip is clearly a better match for this particular data. Compression almost quadrupled our effective disk space. While that's fairly impressive, let's turn up the volume.

```
# zfs set compress=gzip-9 db/text
# cp /home/mwl/hgp.txt /db/
# du /db/hgp.txt
63614    /db/hgp.txt
```

Cranking up the compression to gzip-9 reduces this 274 MB file to 62 MB, with a **compressratio** of 4.41. Gzip-9 more than quadruples how much data we can store.

This example cheats, though. Really, really cheats. As in, "writes the formulas on the palm of its hand before the physics test" cheats.

With the exception of the boilerplate added by Project Gutenberg, the Human Genome Project is composed entirely of four letters. It is perhaps the most redundant, most compressible real-world data that exists. You can't expect that from most real-world data.[16]

When to Change Compression Algorithms

Generally, we recommend changing compression algorithms from LZ4 only when a compelling need demands you do so and the additional CPU overhead and slower disk access don't impact actual work.

---

16   Yes, Mr. Pedantic, your real-world data is composed only of ones and zeroes. Go compress your data down to a single 0 and a 1 and see how well that works for you.

Not long ago, Lucas worked for a phone company. The company retained more than a decade of plain-text call detail records (CDRs) for every phone call that had ever been made through their equipment. These records were routinely accessed for running reports in the middle of the night. Occasionally, a fraud investigator needed to access those reports with tools like grep(1) and awk(1). For this use case, enabling gzip-9 compression made perfect sense. Measured with du(1), ZFS compressed the files at roughly 8:1. If we'd needed to routinely interact with these files, however, LZ4 and an extra few hundred dollars in hard drives would have made more sense.

Compression and Performance

Take a look at these properties for the example data.

```
# zfs get all db | grep reference
db/text    referenced         48.7M    -
db/text    logicalreferenced  220M     -
```

This dataset uses 48.7 MB of disk space. When you ignore the compression, the dataset has 220 MB of data. A compressed dataset can store more "logical data" than its size.

Here's where the effectiveness of compression really comes into play. The slowest part of reading and writing data is getting it on the storage media. The physical media is the slowest part of a disk transaction. Writing 48.7 MB to disk takes about 22% as long as writing 220 MB. You can cut your storage times by 78% by enabling compression, at the cost of a little CPU time. If your disk can write 100 MB/s, then writing that 48.7 MB of compressed data will take about half a second. If you look at it from the perspective of the application that wrote the data, you actually wrote 220 MB in half a second, effectively 440 MB/s. We bet you didn't think your laptop disk could manage that!

If you are storing many small files, compression is less effective. Files smaller than the sector size get a whole block allocated to them anyway. If you want really, really effective compression, use a disk with actual 512-byte physical sectors and tell ZFS to use that sector size.

Compression isn't perfect. Sequential and random access can change how well compression performs. Always test with your own data, in your environment. Compression works well enough that FreeBSD enables lz4 compression in its default install.

Most CPUs are mostly idle. Make the lazy critters crunch some data!

Deactivating Compression

To deactivate compression, set the dataset's `compression` property to *off*.

Much as activating compression only affects newly written files, deactivating compression only affects new data. Compressed files remain compressed until rewritten. ZFS is smart enough to know that a file is compressed and to automatically decompress it when accessed, but it still has the overhead.

You cannot purge all traces of compression from a dataset except by rewriting all the files. You're probably better off recreating the dataset.

Deduplication

Files repeat the same data over and over again, arranged slightly differently. Multiple files contain even more repetition. More than half of the data on your system might be duplicates of data found elsewhere. ZFS can identify duplicate data in your files, extract and document it, thus storing each piece of data only once. It's very similar to compression. Deduplication can reduce disk use in certain cases.

Many deduplication systems exist. At one extreme, you could deduplicate all data on a byte-by-byte level. You could deduplicate this book by identifying and recording the position of each letter and punctuation mark, but the record would grow larger than the actual book. At the other extreme, you could deduplicate multiple copies of entire files by recording each only once.

ZFS snapshots could be said to deduplicate filesystem data. For deduplicating files, ZFS deduplicates at the filesystem block level (shown by the `recordsize` property). This makes ZFS good at removing duplicates of identical files, but it realizes that files are duplicates only if their filesystem blocks line up exactly. Using smaller blocks improves how well deduplication works, but increases memory requirements. ZFS stores identical blocks only once and stores the deduplication table in memory.

Enable deduplication on a dataset-by-dataset basis. Every time any file on a deduplicated dataset is accessed by either reading or writing, the system must consult the deduplication table. For efficient deduplication, the system must have enough memory to hold the entire deduplication table. ZFS stores the deduplication table on disk, but if the host must consult the on-disk copy every time it wants to access a file, performance will slow to a drag. (A host must read the dedup table from disk at boot, so you'll get disk thrashing at every reboot anyway.)

While deduplication sounds incredibly cool, you must know how well your data can deduplicate and how much memory deduplication requires before you even consider enabling it.

Deduplication Memory Needs

For a rough-and-dirty approximation, you can assume that 1 TB of deduplicated data uses about 5 GB of RAM. You can more closely approximate memory needs for your particular data by looking at your data pool and doing some math. We recommend always doing the math and computing how much RAM your data needs, then using the most pessimistic result. If the math gives you a number above 5 GB, use your math. If not, assume 5 GB per terabyte.

If you short your system on RAM, performance will plummet like Wile E. Coyote.[17] Don't do that to yourself.

Each filesystem block on a deduplicated dataset uses about 320 bytes of RAM. ZFS' zdb(8) tool can analyze a pool to see how many blocks would be in use. Use the -b flag and the name of the pool you want to analyze.

```
# zdb -b data
Traversing all blocks to verify nothing leaked ...

loading space map for vdev 1 of 2, metaslab 33 of 174
...
5.45G completed ( 341MB/s) estimated time remaining:
      0hr 00min 30sec
```

The "time remaining" counter actually isn't completely terrible, which is good, because the process can run a very long time depending on disk speed and utilization. Once it runs out you'll get a statistical analysis of the pool.

```
bp count:         139025
ganged count:          0
bp logical:    18083569152   avg: 130074
bp physical:   18070658560   avg: 129981 compression:   1.00
bp allocated:  18076997120   avg: 130026 compression:   1.00
bp deduped:             0 ref>1:  0    deduplication:   1.00
SPA allocated: 18076997120  used:  1.81%

additional, non-pointer bps of type 0:      21
Dittoed blocks on same vdev: 1183
```

---

17   Also like Wile E. Coyote, painting a tunnel on the wall won't help.

The "bp count" shows the total number of ZFS blocks stored in the pool. This pool uses 139,025 blocks. While ZFS uses a maximum block size of 128 KB by default, small files use smaller blocks. If a pool has many small files, you'll need more memory.

In the third line from the bottom, the "used" entry shows that this pool is 1.81% (or 0.0181) used. Assume that the data in this pool will remain fairly consistent as it grows. Round up the number of used blocks to 140,000. Divide the used blocks by how full the block is, and we see that the full pool will have about (140,000 / 0.0181 =) 7,734,806 blocks. At 320 bytes per block, this data uses 2,475,138,121 bytes of RAM, or roughly 2.3 GB.

That's less than half the rule of thumb. Assume that the ZFS deduplication table on this pool will need 5 GB of RAM per terabyte of storage.

ZFS lets metadata like the deduplication table take up only 25% of the system's memory. (Actually, it's 25% of the Adaptive Replacement Cache, or ARC, but we'll go into detail on that in *FreeBSD Mastery: Advanced ZFS*.) Each terabyte of deduplicated pool means that the system needs at least 20 GB of RAM. Even if you go with your more hopeful math based on block usage, where each terabyte of disk needs 2.3 GB of RAM, the 25% limit means that each terabyte of deduplicated pool needs about 10 GB of RAM. (In *FreeBSD Mastery: Advanced ZFS*, we discuss adjusting this limit so that people who want to shoot themselves in the foot can do it well.)

Deduplication Effectiveness

ZFS can simulate deduplication and provide a good estimate on how well the data would deduplicate. Run zdb -s on your pool. You'll get a nice histogram of block utilization and common elements, which you can completely ignore in favor of the last line.

```
# zdb -S data
Simulated DDT histogram:
...
dedup = 3.68, compress = 1.00, copies = 1.00,
      dedup * compress / copies = 3.68
```

Our pool data can be deduplicated 3.68 times. If all the data in this pool were this deduplicatable, we could fit 3.68 TB of data in each terabyte of storage. This data is exceptionally redundant, however. For comparison, on Lucas' desktop, the `zroot` pool that contains the FreeBSD operating system, user programs, and home directories, is about 1.06 deduplicatable.

That's not bad. We still need a machine with 20 GB of RAM per terabyte of deduplicated pool, mind you, but we can now make a cost/benefit calculation based on the current needs of hardware. You can also compare your test data's deduplicatability with its compressibility.

Is the memory expense worth it? That depends on the cost of memory versus the cost of storage.

Every time we've assessed our data for deduplicatability and compressibility, and then priced hardware for each situation, we've found that enhancing compression with faster disks and more CPU was more cost-effective than loads of memory for deduplication. Deduplication does not improve disk read speed, although it can improve cache hit rates. It only increases write speed when it finds a duplicate block. Deduplication also significantly increases the amount of time needed to free blocks, so destroying datasets and snapshots can become incredibly slow. Compression affects everything without imposing these penalties.

Deduplication probably only makes sense when disk space is constrained, expensive, and very high performance. If you need to cram lots of deduplicable data onto a pool of SSDs, dedup might be for you.

Everyone's data is different, however, so check yours before making a decision.

Enabling Deduplication

The ZFS property **dedup** activates and deactivates deduplication.

```
# zfs set dedup=on data/data1
```

Deduplication is now active on this data set.

Like compression, deduplication only affects newly written data. Activating deduplication won't magically deduplicate data already on the pool. For best results activate deduplication when first creating the dataset, before writing any data to it.

Disabling Deduplication

To turn deduplication off, set the dataset's **dedup** property to *off*.

```
# zfs set dedup=off data/data1
```

Like compression, disabling deduplication doesn't magically reduplicate all of your files. Deduplicated files remain deduplicated. If you turned off **dedup** because it made system performance abysmal, turning it off won't improve performance. Only removing deduplicated files will improve performance. You can't purge all traces of **dedup** from a dataset. You're better off using zfs send and zfs receive to send the data to a new dataset that doesn't use deduplication.

Your best choice is probably to not use deduplication. Deduplication is a great technology, and the people who need it really do need it. Most of us don't have deduplicable data, however. Don't enable features only because they're cool.

Choosing a disk space management strategy correctly at the beginning will save you much future pain.

Chapter 7: Snapshots and Clones

One of ZFS' most powerful features is snapshots. A filesystem or zvol snapshot allows you to access a copy of the dataset as it existed at a precise moment. Snapshots are read-only, and never change. A snapshot is a frozen image of your files, which you can access at your leisure. While backups normally capture a system across a period of minutes or hours, running backups on a snapshot means that the backup gets a single consistent system image, eliminating those `tar: file changed as we read it` messages and its cousins.

While snapshots are read-only, you can roll the dataset back to the snapshot's state. Take a snapshot before upgrading a system, and if the upgrade goes horribly wrong, you can fall back to the snapshot and yell at your vendor.

Snapshots are the root of many special ZFS features, such as clones. A clone is a fork of a filesystem based on a snapshot. New clones take no additional space, as they share all of their dataset blocks with the snapshot. As you alter the clone, ZFS allocates new storage to accommodate the changes. This lets you spin up several slightly different copies of a dataset without using a full ration of disk space for each. You want to know that your test environment tightly mirrors the production one? Clone your production filesystem and test on the clone.

Snapshots also underpin replication, letting you send datasets from one host to another.

Best of all, ZFS' copy-on-write nature means that snapshots are "free." Creating a snapshot is instantaneous and consumes no additional space.

Copy-on-Write

In both ordinary filesystems and ZFS, files exist as blocks on the disk. In a traditional filesystem, changing the file means changing the file's blocks. If the system crashes or loses power when the system is actively changing those blocks, the resulting shorn write creates a file that's half the old version, half the new, and probably unusable.

ZFS never overwrites a file's existing blocks. When something changes a file, ZFS identifies the blocks that must change and writes them to a new location on the disk. This is called *copy-on-write*, or COW. The old blocks remain untouched. A shorn write might lose the newest changes to the file, but the previous version of the file still exists intact.

Never losing a file is a great benefit of copy-on-write, but COW opens up other possibilities. ZFS creates snapshots by keeping track of the old versions of the changed blocks. That sounds deceptively simple, doesn't it? It is. But like everything simple, the details are complicated. We talked about how ZFS stores data in Chapter 3, but let's go deeper.

ZFS is almost an object-oriented filesystem. Metadata, indexing, and data are all different types of objects that can point to other objects. A ZFS pool is a giant tree of objects, rooted in the pool labels.

Each disk in a pool contains four copies of the ZFS label: two at the front of the drive and two at the end. Each label contains the pool name, a Globally Unique ID (GUID), and information on each member of the VDEV. Each label also contains 128 KB for uberblocks.

The uberblock is a fixed size object that contains a pointer to the Meta Object Set (MOS), the number of the transaction group that generated the uberblock, and a checksum.

The MOS records the top-level information about everything in the pool, including a pointer to a list of all of the root datasets in the pool. In turn each of these lists points to similar lists for their children, and to blocks that describe the files and directories stored in the dataset. ZFS chains these lists and pointer objects as needed for your data. At the bottom of the tree, the leaf blocks contain the actual data stored on the pool.

Every object contains a checksum and a birth time. The checksum is used to make sure the object is valid. The birth time is the transaction group (txg) number that created the block. Birth time is a critical part of snapshot infrastructure.

Modifying a block of data touches the whole tree. The modified block of data is written to a new location, so the block that points to it is updated. This pointer block is also written to a new location, so the next object up the tree needs updating. This percolates all the way up to the uberblock.

The uberblock is the root of the tree. Everything descends from it. ZFS can't modify the uberblock without breaking the rules of copy-on-write, so it rotates the uberblock. Each label reserves 128 KB for uberblocks. Disks with 512-byte sectors have 128 uberblocks, while disks with 4 KB sectors have 32 uberblocks. If you have a disk with 16 KB sectors, it will have only eight uberblocks. Each filesystem update adds a new uberblock to this array. When the array fills up, the oldest uberblock gets overwritten.

When the system starts, ZFS scans all of the uberblocks, finds the newest one with a valid checksum, and uses that to import the pool. Even if the most recent update somehow got botched, the system can import a consistent version of what the pool was like a few seconds before that. If the system failed during a write, the very last data is lost—but that data never made it to disk anyway. It's gone, and ZFS can't help you. Using copy-on-write means that ZFS doesn't suffer from the problems that make `fsck(8)` necessary for traditional filesystems.

How Snapshots Work

When the administrator tells ZFS to create a snapshot, ZFS copies the filesystem's top-level metadata block. The live system uses the copy, leaving the original for use by the snapshot. Creating the snapshot requires copying only the one block, which means that ZFS can create snapshots almost instantly. ZFS won't modify data or metadata inside the snapshot, making snapshots read-only. ZFS does record other metadata about the snapshot, such as the birth time.

Snapshots also require a new piece of ZFS metadata, the dead list. A dataset's dead list records all the blocks that were used by the most recent snapshot but are no longer part of the dataset. When you delete a file from the dataset, the blocks used by that file get added to the dataset's dead list. When you create a snapshot, the live dataset's dead list is handed off to the snapshot and the live dataset gets a new, empty dead list.

Deleting, modifying, or overwriting a file on the live dataset means allocating new blocks for the new data and disconnecting blocks containing old data. Snapshots need some of those old data blocks, however. Before discarding an old block, the system checks to see if a snapshot still needs it.

ZFS compares the birth time of the old data block with the birth time of the most recent snapshot. Blocks younger than the snapshot can't possibly be used by that snapshot and can be tossed into the recycle bin. Blocks older than the snapshot birth time are still used by the snapshot, and so get added to the live dataset's dead list.

After all this, a snapshot is merely a list of which blocks were in use in the live dataset at the time the snapshot was taken. Creating a snapshot tells ZFS to preserve those blocks, even if the files that use those blocks are removed from the live filesystem.

This means that ZFS doesn't keep copies of every version of every file. When you create a new file and delete it before taking a snapshot, the file is gone. Each snapshot contains a copy of each file as it existed when the snapshot was created. ZFS does not retain a history like DragonFly's HAMMER.

Deleting a snapshot requires comparing block birth times to determine which blocks can now be freed and which are still in use. If you delete the most recent snapshot, the dataset's current dead list gets updated to remove blocks required only by that snapshot.

Snapshots mean that data can stick around for a long time. If you took a snapshot one year ago, any blocks with a birth date more than a year ago are still in use, whether you deleted them 11 months ago or before lunch today. Deleting a six-month-old snapshot might not free up much space if the year-old snapshot needs most of those blocks.[18]

Only once no filesystems, volumes, or snapshots use a block, does it get freed.

---

18   Snapshots make you the data equivalent of a hoarder. Do try to not get buried in an avalanche of old newspapers.

Using Snapshots

To experiment with snapshots, let's create a new filesystem dataset and populate it with some files.

```
# zfs create -o mountpoint=/sheep mypool/sheep
# cd /sheep
# dd if=/dev/random of=randomfile bs=1m count=1
# fetch -o zfsbook.html http://www.zfsbook.com/
# date > date.txt
```

This gives us some data we can play with.

Creating a Snapshot

Use `zfs snapshot` to create a snapshot. Specify the dataset by its full path, then add @ and a snapshot name.

```
# zfs snapshot mypool/sheep@snap1
```

View snapshots with `zfs list -t snapshot`. To see the snapshots of a specific dataset, add the `-r` flag and the dataset name.

```
# zfs list -t snapshot -r mypool/sheep
NAME                  USED   AVAIL   REFER   MOUNTPOINT
mypool/sheep@snap1     0       -     1.11M   -
```

Notice that the amount of space used by the snapshot (the USED column) is 0. Every block in the snapshot is still used by the live dataset, so the snapshot uses no additional space.

Dataset Changes and Snapshot Space

Now change the dataset and see how it affects the snapshots. Here we append a megabyte of new crud to the random file and update the date file.

```
# dd if=/dev/random of=randomfile bs=1m count=1 oseek=1
# date > date.txt
```

Think back on how snapshots work. The file of random data grew by one megabyte, but that's not in the old snapshot. The date file was replaced, so the snapshot should have held onto the blocks used by the older file. Let's see what that does to the snapshot's space usage.

```
# zfs list -t snapshot -r mypool/sheep
NAME                     USED  AVAIL  REFER  MOUNTPOINT
mypool/sheep@snap1       72K      -   1.11M  -
```

The snapshot now uses 72 KB. The only space consumed by the snapshot was for the replaced block from the date file. The snapshot doesn't get charged for the new space sucked up by the larger random file, because no blocks were overwritten.

Now let's create a second snapshot and see how much space it uses.

```
# zfs snapshot mypool/sheep@second
# zfs list -t snapshot -r mypool/sheep
NAME                     USED  AVAIL  REFER  MOUNTPOINT
mypool/sheep@snap1       72K      -   1.11M  -
mypool/sheep@second       0       -   2.11M  -
```

The REFER column shows that the first snapshot gives you access to 1.11 MB of data, while the second lets you see 2.11 MB of data. The first snapshot uses 72 KB of space, while the second uses none. The second snapshot is still identical to the live dataset.

But not for long. Let's change the live dataset by overwriting part of the random file and see how space usage changes.

```
# dd if=/dev/random of=randomfile bs=1m count=1 oseek=1
# zfs list -t snapshot -r mypool/sheep
NAME                     USED  AVAIL  REFER  MOUNTPOINT
mypool/sheep@snap1       72K      -   1.11M  -
mypool/sheep@second    1.07M      -   2.11M  -
```

We've overwritten one megabyte of the random data file. The first snapshot's space usage hasn't changed. The second snapshot shows that it's using 1 MB of space to retain the overwritten data, plus some metadata overhead.

Recursive Snapshots

ZFS lets you create recursive snapshots, which take a snapshot of the dataset you specify and all its children. All of the snapshots have the same name. Use the -r flag to recursively snapshot a system. Here we snapshot the boot pool with a single command.

```
# zfs snapshot -r zroot@beforeupgrade
```

We now have a separate snapshot for each dataset in this pool, each tagged with @beforeupgrade.

```
# zfs list -t snapshot
NAME                              USED  AVAIL  REFER
MOUNTPOINT
zroot@beforeupgrade                 0     -    144K   -
zroot/ROOT@beforeupgrade            0     -    144K   -
zroot/ROOT/default@beforeupgrade    0     -    1.35G  -
zroot/usr@beforeupgrade             0     -    454M   -
zroot/usr/local@beforeupgrade       0     -    1.54G  -
...
```

We can now abuse this system with wild abandon, secure in knowing that a known good version of the system exists in snapshots.

Advanced Dataset and Snapshot Viewing

Once you grow accustomed to ZFS you'll find that you've created a lot of datasets, and that each dataset has a whole bunch of snapshots. Trying to find the exact snapshots you want gets troublesome. While you can always fall back on grep(1), the ZFS command line tools have very powerful features for viewing and managing your datasets and snapshots. Combining options lets you zero in on exactly what you want to see. We started with zfs list in Chapter 4, but let's plunge all the way in now.

Many of these options work for other types of datasets as well as snapshots. If you stack filesystems 19 layers deep, you'll probably want to limit what you see. For most of us, though, snapshots are where these options really start to be useful. Many features also work with zpool(8) and pools, although pools don't get as complicated as datasets.

A plain `zfs list` displays filesystem and zvol datasets, but no snapshots.

```
# zfs list
NAME                    USED    AVAIL   REFER   MOUNTPOINT
mypool                  4.62G   13.7G   96K     none
mypool/ROOT             469M    13.7G   96K     none
mypool/ROOT/default     469M    13.7G   469M    /
mypool/avolume          4.13G   17.8G   64K     -
...
```

You can examine a single dataset by name.

```
# zfs list mypool/sheep
NAME            USED    AVAIL   REFER   MOUNTPOINT
mypool/sheep    2.11M   13.7G   2.11M   /mypool/sheep
```

To view a pool or dataset and all of its children, add the `-r` flag and the pool or dataset name.

```
# zfs list -r mypool/var
NAME                USED    AVAIL   REFER   MOUNTPOINT
mypool/var          22.6G   854G    1.70G   /var
mypool/var/crash    355M    854G    355M    /var/crash
mypool/var/db       224M    854G    187M    /var/db
...
```

Once you get many datasets, you'll want to narrow this further.

View Datasets by Type

To see only a particular type of dataset, use the `-t` flag and the dataset type. You can view filesystems, volumes, snapshots, and bookmarks.

```
# zfs list -t snapshot -r mypool
NAME                        USED    AVAIL   REFER   MOUNTPOINT
mypool@all                  0       -       96K     -
mypool/ROOT@all             0       -       96K     -
mypool/ROOT/default@all     84K     -       419M    -
mypool/avolume@all          0       -       64K     -
...
```

You can examine specific snapshots by giving the complete snapshot name.

```
# zfs list -t snapshot mypool/sheep@all
NAME                USED    AVAIL   REFER   MOUNTPOINT
mypool/sheep@all    0       -       2.11M   -
```

Be sure you give the complete name, including the snapshot part. Here we tell `zfs list` to show only snapshots, and then give it the name of a filesystem dataset; `zfs(8)` very politely tells us to be consistent in what we ask for.

```
# zfs list -t snapshot mypool/sheep
cannot open 'mypool/sheep': operation not applicable to
datasets of this type
```

We used the -r flag before to show a dataset and all of its children. It also works with the list of snapshots.

```
# zfs list -r -t snapshot mypool/second
NAME                        USED  AVAIL  REFER  MOUNTPOINT
mypool/second@all              0      -    96K  -
mypool/second/baby@all         0      -    96K  -
```

To view absolutely everything, use -t all.

```
# zfs list -r -t all mypool/second
NAME                        USED  AVAIL  REFER  MOUNTPOINT
mypool/second               192K  13.5G    96K  legacy
mypool/second@all              0      -    96K  -
mypool/second/baby            96K  13.5G    96K  legacy
mypool/second/baby@all         0      -    96K  -
```

If you have many layers of datasets you might want a partially recursive view. While -r shows all the children, the -d option limits the number of layers you see. Limit the depth to 1 and you get the snapshots of only a single dataset.

```
# zfs list -d 1 -t snapshot mypool/sheep
NAME                        USED  AVAIL  REFER  MOUNTPOINT
mypool/sheep@all               0      -  2.11M  -
mypool/sheep@snap2             0      -  2.11M  -
mypool/sheep@moresnap          0      -  2.11M  -
mypool/sheep@evenmore          0      -  2.11M  -
```

Limiting the depth to 2 would show the specified dataset, snapshots from the specified dataset, and the dataset's children, but not its grandchild filesystems or its children's snapshots.

Modifying zfs list Output

You can control which information `zfs list` displays with the `-o` option and a list of columns or properties. When you use `-o`, `zfs list` displays only the information you request.

Look at any of the earlier `zfs list` output and you'll see that the NAME column (predictably) shows the dataset name. Show only that column with `-o`. Here we recursively list all of the snapshots in *mypool*, showing only their name.

```
# zfs list -r -t snapshot -o name mypool
NAME
mypool@all
mypool/ROOT@all
mypool/sheep@snap2
mypool/sheep@moresnap
mypool/sheep@evenmore
...
```

You can display any property as a column as well. Here we list some common filesystem properties for each dataset.

```
# zfs list -o name,atime,exec,setuid
NAME            ATIME  EXEC  SETUID
mypool            on    on     on
mypool/sheep      on    on     on
zroot            off    on     on
zroot/ROOT       off    on     on
```

Yes, filesystem properties have nothing to do with snapshots. But they're a good example of this feature.

Finally, you can change the order `zfs list` shows datasets. Use `-s` and a property to sort by the property's value. Use `-s` and a property to reverse sort the output by the property. List multiple properties in order, separated by commas.

Listing Snapshots by Default

The `zfs list` command defaults to hiding snapshots and bookmarks. If you want to see these datasets by default, set the pool's **listsnapshots** property to *on*.

```
# zpool set listsnapshots=on zroot
```

Once you've run with this for a while, however, we're highly confident you'll turn it back off. Accumulated snapshots quickly overwhelm everything else.

Scripts and ZFS

Sysadmins like automation. One annoying thing about automation is when you must run a command and parse the output. Making output more human-friendly often makes it less automation-friendly. The ZFS developers were all too familiar with this problem, and included command-line options to eliminate most of it.

The -p option tells zfs(8) and zpool(8) to print exact values, rather than human-friendly ones. A pool doesn't actually have 2 TB free—it's just a number that rounds to that. Using p prints the actual value in all its glory.

The -H option tells zfs(8) and zpool(8) to not print headers, and to separate columns with a single tab, instead of making them line up nicely, the way humans like. You are human, aren't you?

Combined together, these options transform output from something easily understood by humans to something you can feed straight to a script.

```
# zfs list -t all -pH -r mypool
mypool  2670592  96529122918498304   /mypool
mypool/sheep  2351104 965291229184 2273280 /sheep
mypool/sheep@snap1  77824   -  1224704 -
mypool/sheep@second 0   -  2273280 -
...
```

Yes, that's the real spacing. Orderly columns are for humans, silly.

Per-Snapshot Space Use

An especially useful property for snapshots is the `written` property, which gives you an idea of how much new data that snapshot contains.

```
# zfs list -d 1 -t all -o name,used,refer,written \
    mypool/sheep
NAME                      USED   REFER   WRITTEN
mypool/sheep             10.3M   6.11M    2.07M
mypool/sheep@all             0   2.11M    2.11M
mypool/sheep@snap2           0   2.11M        0
mypool/sheep@evenmore        0   2.11M        0
mypool/sheep@later       2.07M   5.11M    4.07M
mypool/sheep@rewrite     1.07M   5.11M    2.07M
```

Remember, snapshots appear in order by creation date. The live dataset appears first—while it probably has newer data than any snapshot, it was created before any of its snapshots. The snapshot @all is the oldest, then @snap2, and so on.

The first snapshot, @all, lets you access 2.11 MB of data (the REFER column). This snapshot also contains 2.11 of newly written data. This is the difference between this snapshot and the snapshot before it.

Snapshots @snap2 and @evenmore have no new data. They're unchanged from the first snapshot.

Sometime in between the snapshots @evenmore and @later snapshots, the data grew. The snapshot @later lets you access 5.11 MB of data. It has 4.07 MB of new data.

The @rewrite snapshot also lets you access 5.11 MB of data, but it's written 2.07 MB of new data. As the amount of data you can access is the same as the previous snapshot, some of the old data must have been overwritten.

The live filesystem has also overwritten 1 MB of data. That data is now included only in the @rewrite snapshot.

Accessing Snapshots

The most convenient way to access the content of snapshots is via the *snapshot directory*, or *snapdir*. The root of each ZFS dataset has a hidden `.zfs` directory. That directory has a snapshot directory, which in turn has a directory for each snapshot.

```
# ls /mypool/sheep/.zfs
total 1
dr-xr-xr-x  2 root  wheel  2 Mar 29 00:30 shares
dr-xr-xr-x  2 root  wheel  2 Mar 30 16:27 snapshot
# ls -l /mypool/sheep/.zfs/snapshot
total 1
drwxr-xr-x  2 root  wheel  5 Mar 29 00:40 snap1
drwxr-xr-x  2 root  wheel  5 Mar 29 00:40 second
```

Go into that directory and you'll find yourself inside the snapshot's root directory. Each file in the snapshot is preserved exactly as it was when the snapshot was taken, down to the file access time. To recover individual files from a snapshot, copy them back into the main filesystem.

Secret Snapdir

The `.zfs` snapdir is hidden by default. It won't show up even if you run `ls -lA`. This prevents backup programs, `rsync`, and similar software from traversing into it. If you want the `.zfs` directory to show up, set the dataset's **snapdir** property to *visible*.

```
# zfs set snapdir=visible mypool/sheep
```

Once someone runs `cp -R` on a dataset, recursively copies all your snapshots onto the filesystem, and blows everything up, hide it again by setting the **snapdir** property to *hidden*.

Mounting Snapshots

You can mount a snapshot much like you'd mount any other filesystem.

```
# mount -t zfs mypool/sheep@snap1 /mnt
```

You cannot access a snapshot via the hidden `.zfs` directory while it is manually mounted. Even a mounted snapshot is still read-only.

Deleting Snapshots

Snapshots prevent the blocks they use from being freed. This means you don't get that space back until you stop using those blocks, by removing all snapshots that reference them.

Create a new snapshot, and then remove it:

```
# zfs snapshot mypool/sheep@deleteme
# zfs destroy mypool/sheep@deleteme
```

That wasn't so hard, was it?

You can also add the verbose flag (`-v`), to get more detail about what's being destroyed. While verbose mode doesn't help much when you're destroying a single snapshot, it becomes more valuable as you destroy more datasets or if you want to see what a command would do without actually running it.

Destruction Dry Runs

The `noop` flag, `-n`, does a "dry run" of the delete process. It describes what would happen if you delete the snapshot without actually deleting it. Let's return to those first few snapshots we took and see what would happen if we removed the first one.

```
# zfs destroy -vn mypool/sheep@snap1
would destroy mypool/sheep@snap1
would reclaim 72K
```

Deleting this snapshot would reclaim only 72 KB of space. The blocks that make up this snapshot are still used by the live filesystem and/or the second snapshot.

Our second snapshot overwrote some of the data from the first snapshot. That changes the effect of deleting the snapshot.

```
# zfs destroy -vn mypool/sheep@second
would destroy mypool/sheep@second
would reclaim 1.07M
```

We would free the space used to store the overwritten version of the files.

Recursion and Ranges

Creating snapshots recursively can create a whole mess of snapshots. Fortunately, you can recursively destroy snapshots as well.

```
# zfs destroy -rv mypool@all
will destroy mypool@all
will destroy mypool/second@all
will destroy mypool/second/baby@all
will destroy mypool/lamb@all
will destroy mypool/ROOT@all
...
will reclaim 84K
```

Recursively destroying snapshots is a great time to use -n before actually destroying any data.[19] More than once, we've realized that we need a snapshot two seconds after deleting it.

Another handy feature is destroying a range of snapshots. You give two snapshots of the same dataset, and ZFS wipes them out and all snapshots taken between them. Run `zfs destroy`, but give the full name of the "from" snapshot, a percent sign, and the name of the "to" snapshot. Those two snapshots and everything between them get destroyed.

The -n flag is handy to make sure this is going to do what you expect before you actually execute it. Plus you learn how much space you'll get back.

---

19   When shooting yourself in the foot, aim carefully. Safety first!

Here, we destroy our two test snapshots. Note that the first snapshot is given by its full name, including the dataset: *mypool/sheep@my-firstsnapshot*. The second snapshot has to be part of the same dataset, and it has to be a snapshot, so you need only the brief name of the snapshot: *second*.

```
# zfs destroy -vn mypool/sheep@snap1%second
would destroy mypool/sheep@snap1
would destroy mypool/sheep@second
would reclaim 1.14M
```

If you are sure, drop the -vn and truly destroy the snapshots:

```
# zfs destroy mypool/sheep@snap1%second
```

The snapshots are gone. Your users are now free to tell you that they needed that data.

Rolling Back

Snapshots don't only show you how the filesystem existed at a point in the past. You can revert the entire dataset to its snapshot state. Going to do an upgrade? Create a snapshot first. If it doesn't work, just roll back. Use the zfs rollback command to revert a filesystem to a snapshot. But once you go back, you can't go forward again.

Here we create a filesystem with a series of changes, snapshotting each one.

```
# zfs create -o mountpoint=/delorean mypool/delorean
# echo "this is the past" > /delorean/timecapsule.txt
# zfs snapshot mypool/delorean@thepast
# echo "this is the present" > /delorean/timecapsule.txt
# zfs snapshot mypool/delorean@thepresent
# echo "I broke the future" > /delorean/timecapsule.txt
```

The file */delorean/timecapsule.txt* has had three different sets of text in it. Two versions of that text are captured in snapshots. The third is not in a snapshot.

```
# cat /delorean/timecapsule.txt
"I broke the future"
```

Oh no, the future is broken. Let's return to the present. Run `zfs rollback` and give the name of the snapshot you want to use.

```
# zfs rollback mypool/delorean@thepresent
```

This takes less time than you might think. Remember, all the data and metadata is already on disk. ZFS only switches which set of metadata it uses. Once the rollback finishes, the live filesystem contains all the files from the chosen snapshot.

```
# cat /delorean/timecapsule.txt
"this is the present"
```

Your newer changes to the dataset are gone, and unrecoverable.

While this is a simple example, you can do the exact same thing for a software upgrade, a database migration, or any other risky operation. Operations that once required annoying restorations from offline backup can now be handled in a single command.

You can only roll a filesystem back to the most recent snapshot. It is not possible to surf forwards and backwards like in the movies. If you want to return to an earlier snapshot, "thepast," you must destroy all snapshots newer than your target.

```
# zfs rollback mypool/delorean@thepast
cannot rollback to 'mypool/delorean@thepast': more re-
cent snapshots or bookmarks exist
use '-r' to force deletion of the following snapshots
and bookmarks:
mypool/delorean@thepresent
```

The `zfs rollback` command can destroy all the intermediate snapshots for you if you use the recursive (`-r`) flag. This is not the same kind of multi-dataset recursion used in creating and destroying snapshots. Using `rollback -r` does not roll back the children. You must roll back each dataset separately.

```
# zfs rollback -r mypool/delorean@thepast
# cat /delorean/timecapsule.txt
"this is the past"
```

You've gone back in time, and can now try your risky and painful upgrade again. Congratulations!

Diffing snapshots

Sometimes you really want to know what changed between the time the snapshot was taken and now. If the database server started crashing at noon today, you probably want to compare the state of the filesystem right now with the 11 AM snapshot so you can see if anything changed. You could use find(1) to look for files modified since the snapshot was created, or you could use diff(1) to compare the files from the snapshot with the ones from the live filesystem. ZFS already has this information, however, and makes it available with zfs diff.

To look at the difference between a snapshot and the live filesystem, run zfs diff and give it a snapshot name.

```
# zfs diff mypool/sheep@later
M    /mypool/sheep/randomfile
```

Files can be in four states. A "-" means that the file was removed. A "+" means that the file was added. An "M" indicates that the file has been modified. And an "R" shows that the file has been renamed. Our example here shows that the file /mypool/sheep/randomfile was modified after the snapshot was taken.

You can also compare two snapshots.

```
# zfs diff mypool/sheep@later @muchlater
M   /mypool/sheep/
+   /mypool/sheep/newfile
-   /mypool/sheep/zfsbook.html
R   /mypool/sheep/date.txt -> /mypool/sheep/olddate.txt
M   /mypool/sheep/randomfile
```

The directory */mypool/sheep* was modified. The file */mypool/sheep/newfile* was added, while the file */mypool/sheep/zfsbook.html* was removed. We have a file rename and, again, the file *randomfile* was modified.

You can also get even more detail. If you add the -t flag, the output includes the change's timestamp from the inode. The -F flag includes the type of the file. Check zfs(8) to get the full list of file types.

Automatic Snapshot Regimen

Snapshots are useful even if you create them only for special events. If you create snapshots automatically on a schedule, however, they become extremely useful. It's simple enough to schedule creating a recursive snapshot of your system every 15 minutes. If you keep all of these snapshots, your pool fills up, however. Automated snapshots need rotating and discarding just like backup tapes.

Rotation Schedule

The hard part of scheduling the creation and destruction of snapshots is figuring out how you might use the snapshots. Who are your users? What applications might need snapshots? We can't answer those questions for you.

One common setup is built around weekly, daily, hourly, and 15-minute snapshots. You take weekly snapshots that you keep for two months. Daily snapshots are retained for two weeks. Your hourly snapshots are retained for three days. Then you take snapshots every 15 minutes and keep those for six hours.

Maybe you need only four 15-minute snapshots. Or you must retain monthly snapshots for a year. The regimen right for you depends on many factors. How important is your data? How far back might you have to reach? How space constrained are you? How often do your files change, and how much new data gets written each day? Do you have IT audit controls that dictate how long certain data must be retained? Talk with other people on your team, and figure out a schedule that works for your organization.

Once you have your desired schedule, ZFS tools can help you deploy it.

ZFS Tools

Many scripts and software packages can manage ZFS snapshots for you. We recommend *ZFS Tools* (https://github.com/bdrewery/zfstools), as it doesn't use a configuration file. It does need `cron(8)`, but you don't have to mess with any kind of `zfstools.conf`. ZFS Tools takes its configuration from user-defined properties set within ZFS. This means that new datasets automatically inherit their snapshot configuration from their parent. When a system has dozens of datasets and you're constantly creating and removing them, inherited configuration saves lots of time.

Install ZFS Tools from packages.

```
# pkg install zfstools
```

ZFS Tools come with many scripts and applications, but right now we're concerned with `zfs-auto-snapshot`.

zfs-auto-snapshot

The `zfs-auto-snapshot` Ruby script creates and deletes snapshots. It takes two arguments, the name of the snapshot, and the number of those snapshots to keep. For example, running `zfs-auto-snapshot frequent 4` creates a recursive snapshot named *frequent*, and keeps four snapshots of each dataset.

Combined with `cron(8)`, `zfs-auto-snapshot` lets you create whatever snapshots you like, at any time interval desired, and then discard them as they age out.

ZFS Tools come with a default crontab to create snapshots on a schedule that the developers hope will fit most people's needs. It starts by setting $PATH so that `zfs-auto-snapshot` can find Ruby. It then has entries to create 15-minute, hourly, daily, weekly, and monthly snapshots. Let's look at each.

```
15,30,45 * * * * root /usr/local/sbin/zfs-auto-snapshot frequent 4
```

`zfs-auto-snapshot` runs on the 15th, 30th, and 45th minute of each hour. It creates a snapshot called *frequent* on each dataset. When a dataset has more than four frequent snapshots, the oldest snapshots get removed until only four remain.

```
0    * * * * root /usr/local/sbin/zfs-auto-snapshot hourly   24
```

Every hour, on the hour, `zfs-auto-snapshot` creates a snapshot called *hourly*. It retains 24 of these snapshots, discarding the oldest.

```
7 0 * * * root /usr/local/sbin/zfs-auto-snapshot daily 7
```

Every day, at 7 minutes after midnight, `zfs-auto-snapshot` creates a daily snapshot. It retains seven dailies.

```
14 0 * * 7 root /usr/local/sbin/zfs-auto-snapshot weekly 4
```

On the 7th day of the week, at midnight, `zfs-auto-snapshot` takes a weekly snapshot. It retains four weekly snapshots.

```
28   0 1 * * root /usr/local/sbin/zfs-auto-snapshot monthly  12
```

Monthly snapshots happen on the first day of the month, at 28 minutes past midnight. We keep 12 of them.

These crontab entries are designed for */etc/crontab*. If you use them in root's crontab, you must remove the user (root) entry from each. In either case, be sure to include the PATH variable so zfs-auto-tools can find Ruby.

Adjust the names and schedules to fit your environment and prejudices. Lucas always renames the *frequent* snapshots to *15min*, because the word *frequent* is ambiguous. But he's kind of a pain, so ignore what he thinks.

Enabling Automatic Snapshots

The `zfs-auto-snapshot` script only creates snapshots of datasets that have the **com.sun:auto-snapshot** property set to *true*. Datasets without this property, or that have it set to any value other than true, will not get snapshotted. Setting this property on a dataset lets all of the child datasets inherit it.

Here we set **com.sun:auto-snapshot** on the root dataset of the pool *mypool*.

```
# zfs set com.sun:auto-snapshot=true mypool
```

When `zfs-auto-snapshot` runs, it creates snapshots of every dataset in *mypool*, with the name and intervals dictated by */etc/crontab*.

Some datasets probably don't need snapshots. We never snapshot the ports tree, for example. To turn off snapshots for a dataset and its children, set **com.sun:auto-snapshot** to *false*.

```
# zfs set com.sun:auto-snapshot=false mypool/usr/ports
```

You can also disable just specific classes of snapshots. A dataset that doesn't change frequently probably doesn't need frequent or hourly snapshots. `zfs-auto-snapshot` checks for sub-properties of **com. sun:auto-snapshot** named after the snapshot period. For example, the property that controls your hourly snapshots is named **com. sun:auto-snapshot:hourly**. Set these properties to *false* to disable those snapshots.

```
# zfs set com.sun:auto-snapshot:frequent=false mypool/delorean
# zfs set com.sun:auto-snapshot:hourly=false mypool/delorean
```

Now `zfs-auto-snapshot` only takes daily, weekly, and monthly snapshots for that dataset and all of its children. You can re-enable the more frequent snapshots for a specific child by setting the property back to *true* on that child.

You may also decide that, while you need frequent snapshots of */usr/src* since you are working on some important code, you don't need to keep months-old copies of the source tree:

```
# zfs set com.sun:auto-snapshot:monthly=false mypool/usr/src
```

ZFS Tools' `zfs-auto-snapshot` handles all snapshot rotation for you.

Viewing Automatic Snapshots

Automatic snapshots have names beginning with zfs-auto-snap and followed by the period and the timestamp.

```
# zfs list -t all -r db/db
NAME                                            USED  AVAIL  REFER
MOUNTPOINT
db/db                                           587M  13.5G  561M   /
db/db@zfs-auto-snap_hourly-2015-04-08-16h00     224K  -      561M   -
db/db@zfs-auto-snap_hourly-2015-04-08-17h00     220K  -      561M   -
db/db@zfs-auto-snap_hourly-2015-04-08-18h00     200K  -      561M   -
db/db@zfs-auto-snap_frequent-2015-04-08-18h45   188K  -      561M   -
db/db@zfs-auto-snap_hourly-2015-04-08-19h00     172K  -      561M   -
db/db@zfs-auto-snap_frequent-2015-04-08-19h15   172K  -      561M   -
db/db@zfs-auto-snap_frequent-2015-04-08-19h30   180K  -      561M   -
db/db@zfs-auto-snap_frequent-2015-04-08-19h45   180K  -      561M   -
db/db@zfs-auto-snap_hourly-2015-04-08-20h00     180K  -      561M   -
```

Getting Clever with zfs-auto-snap

There's nothing magical about the snapshot names or the schedules used by `zfs-auto-snap`. Lucas once ran `zfs-auto-snap hourly 2` at the command line and blew away lots of hourly snapshots. You can name your hourly snapshots *monthly*, and your yearly snapshots *daily*. If you're short on people who detest you and all you stand for, this is a wonderful way to remedy that problem.

Holds

Sometimes, you want a specific snapshot to be retained despite any automatic retention schedule or a desperate late-night effort to clean the pool. Maybe there was an incident, or this is the starting point for some replication. If you need to keep a snapshot, place a hold on it, like your bank does when it doesn't want you to spend your money.

Use `zfs hold`, a tag name, and the snapshot name. A tag name is a human-readable label for this particular hold.

```
# zfs hold tag dataset@snapshot
```

This locks the snapshot and assigns your tag name. One snapshot can have many holds on it, so you can create holds for different purposes.

Holds can also be recursive. To lock all of the snapshots of the same name on child datasets, using a common tag, use `-r`.

```
# zfs hold -r hostages mypool/test@holdme
```

The `zfs holds` command lists the holds on a snapshot, or recursively lists all the holds on a hierarchy of snapshots.

```
# zfs holds -r mypool/test@holdme
NAME                         TAG        TIMESTAMP
mypool/test@holdme           hostages   Fri Apr 3 19:13 2015
mypool/test/sub1@holdme      hostages   Fri Apr 3 19:13 2015
mypool/test/sub2@holdme      hostages   Fri Apr 3 19:13 2015
```

A snapshot with a hold cannot be destroyed.

```
# zfs destroy mypool/test@holdme
cannot destroy snapshot mypool/test@holdme: dataset is busy
```

Release a hold on the dataset with `zfs release`, giving the tag and the dataset name.

```
# zfs release hostages mypool/test@holdme
```

You can now destroy the snapshot. If only getting the bank to release your funds was this easy!

Releasing a hold on a snapshot does not release any hold on its children, however.

```
# zfs destroy -r mypool/test@holdme
cannot destroy snapshot mypool/test/sub1@holdme: dataset is busy
cannot destroy snapshot mypool/test/sub2@holdme: dataset is busy
```

To recursively release all of the holds on a snapshot and its children, use the `-r` flag.

```
# zfs release -r hostages mypool/test@holdme
# zfs destroy -r mypool/test@holdme
```

You can now destroy the child datasets.

Bookmarks

Newer versions of ZFS support *bookmarks*. Bookmarks are similar to snapshots, except they don't keep the old data around. A bookmark is just the timestamp of the snapshot it was created from. Bookmarks are built on the new `extensible_dataset` feature flag.

ZFS requires a timestamp to do incremental replication. ZFS can easily gather up every block that has changed since the bookmark's timestamp. This allows incremental replication, without having to keep the old snapshots around like used to be required.

Bookmarks are a dataset type related to snapshots, so we're mentioning them here. They get full coverage in *FreeBSD Mastery: Advanced ZFS*.

Clones

A clone is a new filesystem created from a snapshot. Initially it uses no new space, sharing all of its blocks with the snapshot that it was created from. While snapshots are read-only, clones are writable like any normal filesystem.

A clone can be thought of as a "fork" or "branch" of a filesystem. If you have a filesystem that contains your web application, you can create a snapshot and clone that snapshot. The cloned filesystem can be your test instance of the application, letting you apply patches and changes without touching the production instance and without consuming extra disk space. You can run tests on the clone version, keeping it running alongside the live version.

Clones do not receive updates made in the original dataset. They're based on a static snapshot. If you want a clone that has your recent updates to the original dataset, you must take a new snapshot and create a new clone.

Clones initially use no disk space. When the clone diverges from the snapshot, any changes made to the cloned filesystem are stored as part of the clone, and it starts to consume space. You might have a multi-terabyte dataset for your big Enterprise Resource Planning (ERP) application, but a fully writable copy of that dataset takes up no space at all except for what you change.

Disk space is already cheap, but clones make it even cheaper.

Creating a Clone

Use `zfs clone` to create a clone. Give it two arguments, the source snapshot and the destination. If your pool has no mount point, you'll need to set one on the clone to access its contents.

```
# zfs clone mypool/sheep@evenmore mypool/dolly
```

Look at our datasets now.

```
# zfs list
NAME                    USED   AVAIL   REFER   MOUNTPOINT
mypool                  4.74G  13.5G    96K    none
...
mypool/sheep            10.3M  13.5G   6.10M   /mypool/sheep
mypool/dolly              8K   13.5G   2.11M   /mypool/dolly
mypool/second           192K   13.5G    96K    legacy
mypool/second/baby       96K   13.5G    96K    legacy
...
```

The *dolly* dataset looks like a normal dataset, except in its space usage. The REFER column shows that it has 2 MB of data, but under USED it takes up only 8 KB. The data it contains is from the original snapshot. A clone consumes space for only newly written data, whether it be new files or overwriting old ones.

Viewing Clones

Clones appear the same as a regular dataset. In zfs list, you won't notice any difference between a clone and any other dataset.[20] Clones record their source snapshot in their **origin** property, however.

```
# zfs get type,origin mypool/dolly
NAME           PROPERTY   VALUE                    SOURCE
mypool/dolly   type       filesystem               -
mypool/dolly   origin     mypool/sheep@evenmore    -
```

So a clone appears, in every way, to just be a regular dataset. The **origin** property is the only way to tell that this is a clone. The origin is the snapshot that this clone was created from.

To track down all of the clones on your system, use zfs list and check the **origin** property. We're checking for any entries that don't end in a dash.

```
# zfs list -o name,origin | grep -ve '-$'
NAME           ORIGIN
mypool/dolly   mypool/sheep@evenmore
```

This gives a list of all datasets that originate in snapshots.

---

20   Clones look like their source material. That's why they make such good assassins. No, wait—wrong clones. Sorry.

Deleting Clones and Snapshots

Clones depend on blocks stored in the source snapshot. The existence of a clone prevents removing the source snapshot. If you try to remove the snapshot, `zfs destroy` tells you there's a problem.

```
# zfs destroy mypool/sheep@evenmore
cannot destroy 'mypool/sheep@evenmore': snapshot has
dependent clones
use '-R' to destroy the following datasets:
mypool/dolly@zfs-auto-snap_frequent-2015-04-08-16h15
mypool/dolly
```

Add the -R flag, and destroying the snapshot takes all the dependent clones with it. You can delete the clone itself like any other filesystem dataset.

```
# zfs destroy mypool/dolly
cannot destroy 'mypool/dolly': filesystem has children
use '-r' to destroy the following datasets:
mypool/dolly@zfs-auto-snap_frequent-2015-04-08-16h15
```

Oh, wait. The clone inherited the **zfs-auto-snapshot** property from its parent, so our snapshot automation caught it. If you didn't want the clone snapshotted, you should have turned that property off. You can manually remove the clone's snapshots, but `zfs-auto-snapshot` keeps creating new ones. You can also use the -r (recursive) flag to destroy the clone and all its snapshots.

```
# zfs destroy -rv mypool/dolly
will destroy mypool/dolly@zfs-auto-snap_frequent-2015-
   04-08-16h15
will destroy mypool/dolly
```

Now we can erase the origin snapshot.

```
# zfs destroy -v mypool/sheep@evenmore
will destroy mypool/sheep@evenmore
will reclaim 0
```

Clones are powerful, but they complicate snapshot management.

Promoting Clones

Now that you've finished testing the developmental version of your web app, you want to make the clone the live version, and discard the previous version. But this causes problems. You cannot destroy the original dataset, because the clone depends on the snapshot from that dataset.

To solve this you "promote" the clone, telling ZFS to reverse the parent/child relationship between the original dataset and the clone. The clone becomes the filesystem. The previous parent becomes a clone. The student becomes the master. Any snapshots that the clone requires move, and become part of the clone instead. Snapshots created after the clone's snapshot of origin still belong to the original parent.

Once the clone successfully switches places with the parent dataset, you can eliminate the original dataset.

ZFS also changes the space used by the new parent and the new clone. The datasets take up no extra space, but the accounting for that space changes. Clones get billed only for the amount of space where they differ from their snapshot of origin. The new parent dataset gets billed for pretty much everything, just like new human parents.

Let's walk through promoting a clone. Here we clone the dataset *mypool/wooly* to a dataset called *mypool/bonnie* and modify the clone.

```
# zfs clone mypool/wooly@later mypool/bonnie
# date > /mypool/bonnie/date.txt
# dd if=/dev/random of=/mypool/bonnie/randomfile bs=1m
count=8 oseek=4
```

Look at the clone's disk usage.

```
# zfs list mypool/bonnie
NAME             USED   AVAIL   REFER   MOUNTPOINT
mypool/bonnie   8.07M   13.5G   12.1M   /mypool/bonnie
```

The USED column shows the 8 MB of new data we wrote to the clone. The REFER column shows the dataset contains 12 MB of data—4 MB from the snapshot of origin, plus the new 8 MB of data we added.

We want to keep the *bonnie* dataset, and get rid of the original *wooly* dataset:

```
# zfs destroy -rv mypool/wooly
cannot destroy 'mypool/wooly': filesystem has dependent
clones
use '-R' to destroy the following datasets:
mypool/bonnie@zfs-auto-snap_frequent-2015-04-08-16h30
mypool/bonnie
```

ZFS knows that the dataset *mypool/bonnie* and its snapshot of origin depend on the *mypool/wooly* dataset. So we use the `zfs promote` command to make *bonnie* the filesystem, and turn the old dataset into the clone.

Before promoting the clone, run `zfs list` and check the space usage and parentage of both datasets involved.

```
# zfs list -t all -r mypool/wooly mypool/bonnie
NAME                          USED   AVAIL   REFER   MOUNTPOINT
mypool/bonnie                 8.07M  13.5G   12.1M   /mypool/
bonnie
mypool/wooly                  10.3M  13.5G   6.10M   /mypool/
sheep
mypool/wooly@all              0      -       2.11M   -
mypool/wooly@moresnap         0      -       2.11M   -
mypool/wooly@later            2.07M  -       5.11M   -
mypool/wooly@rewrite          1.07M  -       5.11M   -
mypool/wooly@muchlater        0      -       6.10M   -
```

We'll come back to this list later. Now promote *mypool/bonnie*.

```
# zfs promote mypool/bonnie
```

The promotion should run silently. Go take a look at these two datasets again.

```
# zfs list -t all -r mypool/wooly mypool/bonnie
NAME                      USED    AVAIL   REFER   MOUNTPOINT
mypool/bonnie             14.3M   13.5G   12.1M   /mypool/
bonnie
mypool/bonnie@all             0       -   2.11M   -
mypool/bonnie@moresnap        0       -   2.11M   -
mypool/bonnie@later       1.07M       -   5.11M   -
mypool/wooly              4.14M   13.5G   4.10M   /mypool/
sheep
mypool/wooly@rewrite      1.07M       -   5.11M   -
mypool/wooly@muchlater        0       -   6.10M   -
```

The snapshot that *mypool/bonnie* was based on, and all snapshots older than that snapshot of origin, now belong to *mypool/bonnie*. Newer snapshots of *mypool/wooly*, taken after the snapshot *mypool/bonnie* was created from, still belong to *mypool/wooly*.

You can now destroy the old dataset and all of its snapshots.

```
# zfs destroy -rv mypool/wooly
will destroy mypool/wooly@muchlater
will destroy mypool/wooly@rewrite
will destroy mypool/wooly
```

Remember that once a clone is forked from the main filesystem, it does not get any updates from the parent. Any persistent data your application needs should go in a different dataset. It can be a child dataset, as Jude prefers. Lucas says that persistent data should go in a completely unrelated dataset, just so a recursive remove doesn't touch it. Watch out for your persistent data in any way you prefer.

Safely Managing Clones, Snapshots, and Recursion

You can take snapshots of datasets. You can create clones based on those snapshots. You can then take snapshots of the clones and create more clones. Despite your best efforts, you're likely to produce a massive tangle of interrelated clones and snapshots that exceed any human's ability to mentally track. ZFS gives you a whole bunch of power and convenience, but clones make possible brand new types of mayhem that will churn your bowels.[21]

The -nv flags are vital to safe systems administration. Any time the merest thought of destroying a dataset begins to consider the possibility of crossing your mind, do a verbose dry run with -nv. See what the destroy command would actually eliminate. Read the list. You might find that your recursive destroy pulls on a thread of clones that stretches all the way across the pool.

Test before you leap. Always.

ZFS changes how you use disk space, but it's still the sysadmin's task to manage it. Let's cover that next.

---

21   Admittedly, the big shoes and red noses don't help. No, wait—that's clowns. Sorry, never mind.

Chapter 8: Installing to ZFS

The whole point of learning about ZFS is to use the filesystem on a machine. Let's discuss FreeBSD 10 installs on ZFS.

If you must install a whole slew of FreeBSD machines, such as at a server farm, we recommend the PC-BSD installer. Scripts like we demonstrate here are fine for occasional installs of a few machines, but if you're configuring machines by the rack, you really need a PXE-based installer.

Your hardware limits your choices. With rare exceptions, laptops have one hard drive. Running FreeBSD means using a single striped virtual device pool for storage. If you have hundreds of disks, you'll need to consider how you want to separate your pools.

When you have many many disks, separate your operating system from your data. FreeBSD and a good selection of add-on software fits nicely on a mirrored pool or a RAID-Z. You don't need RAID-Z3 for just the operating system! If you have hundreds of data storage disks, use separate pools for the operating system and data. With hundreds of disks, Lucas would want a few separate pools, but he's an old fogey. Jude would pour them all into one giant pool. The only wrong choice is one that makes more work for you.

This chapter assumes you're familiar with GPT partitioning, FreeBSD tools such as `gpart(8)`, and FreeBSD partition types. If you're not, check the FreeBSD documentation or perhaps read *FreeBSD Mastery: Storage Essentials*. (*FMSE* also covers installation scripts and other advanced installation techniques.)

Installing a ZFS-based system requires configuring storage pools, assigning datasets, and installing FreeBSD to the datasets. You can make separate choices in each step, so we'll consider each separately.

But start with a reference FreeBSD install.

FreeBSD Reference Install

Before installing your custom FreeBSD system, install a small FreeBSD ZFS virtual machine as a reference platform. This offers lots of information about a standard FreeBSD install. Installing your own system is great, but don't abandon all the carefully considered defaults the installer uses. Your goal is probably to tweak the install in a way the installer doesn't permit, not abandon all FreeBSD standards.

Boot your reference platform, become **root**, and run `zpool history` to see how this ZFS was created.

```
# zpool history
History for 'zroot':
2015-04-08.07:18:30 zpool create -o altroot=/mnt -O com-
press=lz4 -O atime=off -m none -f zroot raidz1 da0p3.nop
da1p3.nop da2p3.nop
2015-04-08.07:18:30 zfs create -o mountpoint=none zroot/
ROOT
2015-04-08.07:18:30 zfs create -o mountpoint=/ zroot/
ROOT/default
2015-04-08.07:18:30 zfs create -o mountpoint=/tmp -o ex-
ec=on -o setuid=off zroot/tmp
...
```

We'll use this information throughout the installation process to tweak our install.

Custom ZFS Installation Partitioning

Boot into the FreeBSD installer image, and choose *install*. When you get to the point where you partition disks, select the command line rather than any automatic or guided method. You could also use something like mfsBSD for the version you want, if you have that handy.

Disk Partitioning

When the computer boots, it looks for an operating system on the storage media. For FreeBSD, this is a boot loader. FreeBSD provides the gptzfsboot(8) boot loader specifically for booting from ZFS pools. The hardware BIOS boots the boot loader, which activates the pool and fires up the FreeBSD kernel. Every disk in every virtual device in the boot pool should have a ZFS boot loader installed, which means the disks must be partitioned. The maximum size of the FreeBSD boot loader partition is just a smidgen over 512 KB for some daft reason, so assign 512 KB for the boot loader. Then we put in a 1 GB FreeBSD swap partition, and assign the remaining space for ZFS. The swap and ZFS partitions are aligned at 1 MB boundaries.

While I'm using these short names for the GPT labels for teaching purposes, we strongly encourage you to use location-based labels as discussed in Chapter 0.

```
# gpart add -a 1m -t freebsd-boot -s 512k -l zfsboot da0
da0p1 added
# gpart add -a 1m -t freebsd-swap -s 1g -a 1m -l swap0 da0
da0p2 added
# gpart add -a 1m -t freebsd-zfs -a 1m -l zfs0 da0
da0p3 added
```

Now install the FreeBSD ZFS bootloader onto this disk. Every disk you might boot from needs the bootloader.

```
# gpart bootcode -b /boot/pmbr -p /boot/gptzfsboot -i 1 da0
bootcode written to da0
```

Repeat this partitioning for every disk involved in the storage pool.

Pool Creation

Still at the disk formatting command prompt, assemble your disks into your root storage pool. It's common to call the root pool something like *system* or *zroot*, or you might name it after the host. Do whatever fits for your environment. I'm calling the example pool *zroot*, so that it fits with the default used by the FreeBSD installer.

Look at the default FreeBSD install's `zpool history` and consider what it shows.

```
2015-04-08.07:18:30 zpool create -o altroot=/mnt -O com-
press=lz4 -O atime=off -m none -f zroot raidz1 da0p3.nop
da1p3.nop da2p3.nop
```

This is a FreeBSD 10.1 system. The installer mounts the boot pool temporarily at `/mnt`, and we really have to keep that for the installer to work. We want the other options, like setting **compression** to lz4 and disabling **atime**. The `-m none` tells `zpool(8)` to not assign a mount point to this pool. Using `-f` tells `zpool(8)` to ignore any other ZFS information on these disks. The **altroot** property gives a temporary mount point, as discussed in Chapter 4. You're reinstalling pools, not recycling them.

The 10.1 installer wasn't yet updated to take advantage of the vfs.zfs.min_auto_ashift sysctl, but I'm going to use it now.

```
# sysctl vfs.zfs.min_auto_ashift=12
```

ZFS will now use 4096-byte sectors. Create the pool. We're stealing all of the default FreeBSD options, making only the changes we desire.

```
# zpool create -o altroot=/mnt -O compress=lz4 -O \
    atime=off -m none -f zroot mirror gpt/zfs0 gpt/zfs1 \
    cache gpt/zcache0 log gpt/zlog0
```

Chances are, FreeBSD's default pool installation options are fine. You probably want to tweak the datasets.

Datasets

While you want to create your custom dataset configuration, do check FreeBSD's installation defaults. They're sensible for the average user, and allow use of advanced features like boot environment managers.

If you want to complete your install with the FreeBSD installer, you must give the installer a recognizable system. That means following steps from the reference install, even if you're not sure why a pool is exported and imported at the end of the dataset creation step. In sum, we recommend adding your own datasets, but leaving the defaults unchanged.

Here are a few bits from `zpool history` on a reference FreeBSD host, omitting the timestamps.

```
zfs create -o mountpoint=none zroot/ROOT
zfs create -o mountpoint=/ zroot/ROOT/default
zfs create -o mountpoint=/tmp -o exec=on -o setuid=off
   zroot/tmp
zfs create -o mountpoint=/usr -o canmount=off zroot/usr
zfs create zroot/usr/home
zfs create -o setuid=off zroot/usr/ports
zfs create zroot/usr/src
zfs create -o mountpoint=/var -o canmount=off zroot/var
zfs create -o exec=off -o setuid=off zroot/var/crash
zfs create -o exec=off -o setuid=off zroot/var/log
zfs create -o atime=on zroot/var/mail
zfs create -o setuid=off zroot/var/tmp
zpool set bootfs=zroot/ROOT/default zroot
zpool set cachefile=/mnt/boot/zfs/zpool.cache zroot
```

You can easily add or change your own datasets to this, creating *zroot/var/mysql* or moving */home* out from under */usr* or whatever it is you desire.

Creating datasets is a lot of typing. We recommend creating installation scripts, as discussed in *FreeBSD Mastery: Storage Essentials*.

Once you have your datasets, exit the command-line partitioning and the installer will resume.

Post-Install Setup

Once the installer finishes copying files to your disks, setting up networking, and so on, you'll get a chance to go into the installed system and make changes. Take that chance. You must change a few settings in the finished system.

Make sure that ZFS is started in */etc/rc.conf*. This mounts your filesystem datasets at boot.

```
zfs_enable=yes
```

Edit */boot/loader.conf* to tell FreeBSD to load ZFS and related kernel modules at boot.

```
zfs_load="YES"
```

You can also make any other system changes you like here.

While some documentation refers to other required steps, such as copying the pool cache file, that's no longer necessary.

Reboot when you're finished, and you'll come up in a new, customized FreeBSD install!

Manually Installing FreeBSD

If you have to go to a command line to partition your disks, you might as well install the FreeBSD files to the disk yourself. The FreeBSD distribution files are in */usr/freebsd-dist*, and you write them to your disk with tar(1). Your installation target is mounted in */mnt*.

```
# tar --unlink -xpJf base.txz -C /mnt
# tar --unlink -xpJf kernel.txz -C /mnt
```

You can install other distribution sets, but the base and kernel are the only critical ones.

Your installation needs an */etc/fstab*, for the swap files if nothing else. Create it in */mnt/etc/fstab*. You can also edit critical system files like */mnt/etc/rc.conf* and */mnt/boot/loader.conf*.

With a bit of work and testing, you can make your ZFS install as simple or as complex as you like.

Exactly like you can ZFS.

Afterword

A whole book on a filesystem? Are you mad?

ZFS is merely a filesystem, yes. But it includes features that many filesystems can't even contemplate. You'd never try to wedge self-healing into extfs, or variable block size into UFS2. Copy on write must be built into the filesystem core—you can't retrofit that into an existing filesystem.

By building on decades of experience with filesystems and targeting modern and future hardware, ZFS has not only changed the way we manage digital storage. It's changed how we think about storage. ZFS's flexibility and power has even rendered many long-hallowed "system administration best practices" obsolete. When your filesystem is an ally rather than a menace, everything gets amazingly easier.

The continued growth of OpenZFS brings new features, steady improvement, and a certain future that commercial vendors cannot provide. OpenZFS gets more exciting every week, with new features and greater performance. It also gets less exciting, in that it protects your data more and more with each release. We are fortunate enough to be a part of this great project, and are glad for this chance to share some of our excitement with you.

While Lucas used ZFS before writing this book, Jude uses lots of ZFS to deliver lots of content everywhere in the world. Jude is a FreeBSD doc committer, but Lucas has written big stacks of books. Together, we've created a stronger book than either of us could have alone.

And stay tuned for more ZFS from us. In *FreeBSD Mastery: Advanced ZFS*, we'll take you into strange new filesystem realms unimaginable just a few years ago.

About the Authors

Allan Jude is VP of operations at ScaleEngine Inc., a global Video Streaming CDN, where he makes extensive use of ZFS on FreeBSD.

He is also the host of the weekly video podcasts BSD Now (with Kris Moore) and TechSNAP on JupiterBroadcasting.com. Allan is a FreeBSD committer, focused on improving the documention and implementing libucl and libxo throughout the base system. He taught FreeBSD and NetBSD at Mohawk College in Hamilton, Canada from 2007-2010 and has 13 years of BSD unix sysadmin experience.

Michael W Lucas is a full time author. His FreeBSD experience is almost as old as FreeBSD. He worked for twenty years as a sysadmin

and network engineer at a variety of firms, most of which no longer exist. He's written a whole stack of technology books, which have been translated into nine languages. (Yes, real languages. Ones that people actually speak.) You can find him lurking at various user groups around Detroit, Michigan, his dojo (zenmartialarts.com), or at https://www.michaelwlucas.com.

Find the authors on Twitter as @allanjude and @mwlauthor.

24484175R00131

Made in the USA
Middletown, DE
25 September 2015